PRAISE FOR *TOXICITY*

"This transparent and authentic exploration of a timely and critical topic is exceptional. So often toxic leaders are very good at stake holder management or in other words, disguising their detrimental self serving behaviors behind a facade that they present to senior leadership, enabling them to control the narrative and operate incognito. *Toxicity* provides an accessible playbook that helps identify these destructive traits and enables real change for organizations that are looking for sustainable, repeatable practices based on psychological safety and trust that will build a healthy, thriving company culture wherever they are practiced."

DAN MERRILL - General Manager, LEGO Education

"Too often people just take it. They explain away the bad behavior and the toxic leadership, not even realizing it's WRONG. Hughes masterfully defines toxic leadership and provides guidance on how to manage it and eliminate from your organization!"

DR. JOE ALLEN – Professor of Occupational
Health Psychology, University of Utah

"An accurate depiction (of toxicity) that was very apparent in many of the acquisitions I've lead throughout my 30 plus years in leadership. Extremely insightful and absolutely critical in removing a toxic work environment. An excellent read."

BRUCE WREN – COO, SAS AirCare

"As ethical servant leaders our mandate is to leave the company (and people within the company) better for our stewardship. Bryan's *Culture Recovery Framework* is a strong tool in the toolkit towards this end and worthy of reflective consideration."

PATRICK BRENSINGER – Former President
of a $2B+ Service Company

"Toxic leadership is a topic that everyone talks about, but no one wants to confront. This book tackles it head on with symptoms, diagnosis, and a path to recovery. A must read for those committed to organizational excellence!"

JEFF HORNBERGER – CEO, Residential Real Estate Council

TOXICITY

TOXICITY

LET'S FINALLY DO SOMETHING ABOUT IT

BRYAN C. HUGHES

CLEAR DAY PUBLISHING

TOXICITY: Let's Finally Do Something About It!
Published by Clear Day Publishing
Bountiful, Utah, U.S.A.

HUGHES, BRYAN C., Author
TOXICITY
BRYAN C. HUGHES

Library of Congress Control Number: 2024919967

ISBN: 979-8-9915541-0-7, 979-8-9915541-2-1 (paperback)
ISBN: 979-8-9915541-3-8 (hardcover)
ISBN: 979-8-9915541-1-4 (digital)

BUSINESS & ECONOMICS / Organizational Behavior
BUSINESS & ECONOMICS / Workplace Culture
BUSINESS & ECONOMICS / Human Resources & Personnel Management

Ghostwriter: Danielle Harward (harwardwriting.com)
Book Design: Heidi Caperton (heidicaperton.com)
Publishing Management: Susie Schaefer (finishthebookpublishing.com)

QUANTITY PURCHASES: Schools, companies, professional groups, clubs, and other organizations may qualify for special terms when ordering quantities of this title. For information, email info@clearday-publishing.com

To those who have been impacted by toxicity, or have witnessed toxicity, and are committed to a different way. Cheers to you!

TABLE OF CONTENTS

PART 3
SUSTAINABLE HEALING

Associate:

More commonly known as an "employee", this is an individual who is hired by an organization, or perhaps a volunteer, to achieve common goals. Though "employees" isn't necessarily a negative word, the word "associates" reminds me—and hopefully anyone reading this book—that we all deserve respect.

Follower:

Follower, in this book, is referring to the psychological relationship someone may have with a leader. Toxic, or otherwise.

INTRODUCTION

The great resignation was poorly named. Rather, we all experienced something that I believe should be recognized as the great *reevaluation*.

The switch to remote work during the COVID-19 pandemic gave associates more choices than ever. They were no longer geographically bound to their employers, and they were no longer required to endure environments and the consequences of toxic cultures and leadership. This sparked a wave of departures from environments that failed to foster growth or respect.

In wake of this change, one of the most pressing challenges in corporate America has become associate retention. Yet, even though this is a focal point of discussion, many among executive leadership and human capital practitioners don't know how to address toxic leadership, heal from it, and adjust their culture so that toxic leaders no longer drive their best talent away. In fact, it might be the reason you picked up this book!

Many executives have tried to sell a specific bill of goods to candidates in the talent acquisition process (family environment, development, promotional opportunities) to attract top talent. They hope that this, in part, will help them overcome the toxicity that seems to continually take shape in their companies. However, they often don't make good on those promises. Instead, they only maintain a transactional relationship of trading hours and tasks in return for pay, leaving the associates to fumble in the wake of toxicity and wonder what happened to all those promises made at the door. Today, individuals are more inclined to "move their ladder against another building" if they don't feel those promises have been met or if their development is blocked by a toxic leader.

How do we fix this problem? By addressing the removal and recovery of toxic leaders, and by creating an accountable culture that prevents them from forming in the first place.

Operational excellence in any organization requires a culture of accountability. It should be normalized and integrated into every facet of the organizational framework. In many companies, however, there is a marked absence of accountability culture, both at the organizational and individual levels. Where leaders are as accountable to the associates as the associates are to them. In the absence of this mutual accountability, toxicity builds.

Pushing for operational excellence in the absence of an accountability culture inherently creates a *toxic culture*, where individuals may feel they need to engage in deviant behaviors to accomplish the goals set before them. This stems from a lack of clear expectations and high demands in the absence of a robust feedback loop, making the only clear measure of success the completion of tasks within specific timeframes. When this pressure is not balanced with an accountability culture and ethical guidelines, the stage is set for a breakdown in integrity and safety. This endangers associate well-being and jeopardizes the organization's operational reputation. It fosters a culture where the ends justify the means, which is a direct pathway to ingrained toxic behavior.

Yet, many leaders don't hold themselves accountable to their associates, and might not even hold their associates accountable! In my experience, much of this lack of accountability stems from a misapplication of the servant leadership model. While servant leadership emphasizes the importance of serving others, it should not preclude holding individuals accountable for their performance. Unfortunately, in practice, this leadership style is often overused to the extent that it avoids necessary feedback. Leaders, wary of losing staff, may hesitate to enforce standards or provide feedback at all. When terminations become necessary, these same leaders often find themselves hamstrung by insufficient documentation or a lack of validated coaching.

Sadly, in my academic research and professional practice, I have found many terminated associates report in exit interviews that their first real coaching session occurred only shortly before their termination! In an effort to avoid the risk of being sued for wrongful termination—due to lack of a paper trail—human capital and operational leaders may opt to keep the associate on, which allows the behaviors to fester and is seen by others as an approval.

All of this deeply affects a company's culture and creates a prime breeding ground for toxicity. Organizations attempt to remedy these failures with superficial measures such as hosting social events like pizza parties, tweaking compensation plans, or conducting associate surveys with basic questions like "Would you recommend working here?" or "Do you feel like you are heard?" to try and gauge how associates feel about those they report to, without following up with sufficient measures to improve conditions.

While these initiatives are not inherently flawed, their implementation lacks depth. This is especially true because prestige-driven toxic leaders can artificially inflate survey scores by incentivizing positive feedback or by using threats and guilt to silence dissent. This manipulation can lead to a skewed understanding of associate satisfaction and organizational culture by executive leadership. Those associates who doubt themselves may score the organization higher out of fear or pressure, while dissenters may opt out of completing the survey altogether due to a lack of trust.

Unfortunately, in many organizations, not only do these challenges exist, but they are the status quo.

Then executive leadership becomes frustrated when toxicity continues to appear. What's worse, if they do get rid of a toxic leader, they sweep the termination under the rug because they are embarrassed such toxic leaders occurred under their watch. They don't help the teams affected heal from the toxicity, and they don't take steps to stop future toxicity.

If you remove a toxic leader, yet don't make any cultural changes, you haven't stopped toxicity. Just like when you try to lose weight, you can jog all the time, but if you don't adjust your diet to healthier foods, you won't see any changes. The book *Good to Great*, by Jim Collins, introduced the "Flywheel Effect."[1] This is the idea that successful organizational momentum takes time and many small acts. And once the momentum—through these small progressive acts—is established, it becomes a continuous cycle of success for the company. An organization may remove a toxic leader and do nothing else while often believing they are adding to the momentum of the flywheel. Yet they aren't. They are more likely only running on a "hamster wheel" instead, exerting tremendous effort without making any real progress.

All this to say, whether you are operating within the tech industry on the West Coast, manufacturing in the Midwest, or finance on the East Coast, the challenges of toxic leadership and the mainstream tactics to overcome it (which don't typically work), remain consistent. Toxicity can manifest in any company. It knows no boundaries. Even in scenarios where overtly toxic leaders are not present, an organizational framework that fails to curb negative influences can create an environment ripe for toxicity, and toxicity has a high opportunity cost for your company.

Organizations spend considerable resources managing dismissals and replacements. When toxicity breeds deviant behaviors such as fraud, theft, manipulation, and triangulation, these costs only increase. Not to mention the obvious legal repercussions that could come from these behaviors. Plus, cultures full of toxicity will stifle innovation. Especially if the culture becomes one where "credit" is the central focus, associates might withhold their innovative ideas, fearing they won't receive due recognition. Or worse, they may leave the organization to seek an environment that they believe will deliver greater value and encouragement of their contributions.

There is an ethical *and* operational advantage to addressing toxicity. But you must commit to making the change, and it is crucial to know the correct changes to make. With this book, I aim to show you how.

With now nearly three decades of professional experience, with two decades in executive leadership roles, I have seen many business models and worked in several different capacities. I have worked for, consulted, or advised organizations in every North American time zone; and in nearly all the companies I've consulted for, I have seen the toxicity they so desperately wish to remove. Through my experience, I have cultivated a framework that will instill accountability and trust within your organization so it can heal from, and deter, toxicity.

How did I come up with this framework? After two decades of leadership, I began pursuing my doctorate and had the opportunity to conduct academic research on toxic leadership. For my dissertation, I took my experience and measured it against the research I conducted. I chose culture recovery as the topic because through my professional experience, I found that operational tweaks can result in minor improvements, but they rarely lead to sustainable growth or significant change. Often, the main blocker of operational excellence was deeper, embedded in the leadership styles and the organizational culture.

The result of this study created a researched-backed framework to heal pervasive toxicity in organizations and to ultimately increase associate retention. Then, for the past several years, I have tried and tested this framework in companies across America. The results? I have successfully used these methods to help my clients heal their culture and remove toxicity. Everything I discuss is grounded in science, peer-reviewed and published,[2] and applied through my experience in the practical realities of organizational leadership. This framework is tried and tested. If you follow it, you will see results.

My hope is that with this book, executive leaders and human capital practitioners will expand their vision and thinking around culture development and use the Culture Recovery Framework to move away from the all-too-common pervasive toxicity many organizations face. Leaders have a moral and ethical obligation to cultivate an environment where associates feel genuinely valued and see opportunities for personal growth. But what's more, this framework is the solution to the associate retention problem many organizations face. It is the answer to why toxicity continues to grow within your organization, and it will help you create a culture that ethical and talented associates seek to join.

I have seen these methods work time and time again and will provide you with case studies of how they affected change within the organizations I have worked with. After-all, who doesn't need a little proof in the pudding? When preparing for this work, I considered the organizations I have had experience with. Every one of these groups was filled with people, just like you and me. This book is about human connection and interaction, but you will notice that my stories are often more general. I want to help improve things, and calling individuals to account publicly will not assist in this. So, when I speak of experiences with organizations, know that I am thinking about the very humans in those spaces, and I hope this serves to improve the conditions for each.

Reading this book *alone* will not fix the issues in your organization. Yet, by reading this book and applying these principles on a consistent basis, you will see significant and sustainable results. All it takes is a commitment to do something different tomorrow.

Are you ready?

PART
1

BREAKING TRADITIONAL PATTERNS

everal years ago, I was asked to work with an organization to help them integrate a newly acquired company into a larger national corporation. I've done this on several occasions.

This was a several-decade old organization, acquiring an even older firm. The primary organization's goal was to realize significant results through efficiencies and scale, yet to not lose brand equity or experience client and staff churn. Essentially, the object was to realize exponential growth, but without changing a thing!

On paper, both firms were high performing in their space. One national, the other regional, each had the respect of industry peers and clients. While each had their unique strengths and weaknesses, both suffered from hidden toxic senior leaders with their own interests as their primary motivation.

Don't get me wrong, these were not broken companies. They had many metrics showing you how great they were, and they publicly advertised these scores every chance they had. These were metrics showing their client satisfaction, their associate satisfaction, and their year-over-year growth. It was all very impressive, yet they couldn't quite break away from the status quo when it came to organic growth. Certainly, they could buy growth through acquisition, but they were stagnant despite their respective professional sales and marketing teams.

As I spent time with the teams from both organizations, I quickly realized that they both suffered from various consequences of toxic leadership. With the newly acquired company, it was more of a shared culture than a single leader. The former owner was very well respected, and it was known and observed that they cared for the firm and the people, but they were somewhat aloof from the day-to-day aspects. They preached a family environment, and perhaps in many cases that could be validated. But the judgements of success were tied to metrics around client-deliverables, and unfortunately didn't include measures of organizational health. This unintentionally allowed certain individuals to shift from acting for the betterment of the organization to acting towards their own personal interests.

Over the proceeding months, we found several issues of fraud, falsely counting customers and resources, and intentional efforts by these toxic individuals to surround themselves with individuals who were like-minded and who would support their actions. These offending individuals weren't overtly hostile or abusive though. They would publicly claim to follow the organizational objectives and spirit. However, their self-interested behaviors would consequently lead to an overarching toxicity in the workplace. Meanwhile, those who felt that they could no longer align with what felt like a hypocrite culture left the organization. Without an appropriate sense of self-awareness, senior leadership simply assumed that these departed individuals weren't a fit for the team or weren't loyal, and they never gave it further consideration.

The acquiring company had many of the same challenges, but I found that these toxic leaders were more likely bound within certain geographic or division constraints. When the actions of these toxic leaders became gross enough that they affected the business performance, or perhaps complaints registered at corporate levels, action would finally be taken. The local leader was removed and replaced with someone else. Nothing else would happen. The larger organization would make no comments to the affected team, and there would be no open dialogue with the individuals who felt abused.

Because the organization utilized many resources to evaluate the leadership candidate and their tendencies towards toxicity without finding anything, they assumed this circumstance was a unique outlier and something they simply could not have avoided. Yet, even with the former leader gone, the team and the culture did not heal. The stings of divisiveness and personal agendas and vendettas had cast aside any sense of team spirit. Because of the lack of organizational trust as a consequence of the previous leader, the team had difficulty aligning with the new leadership vision.

Even if there were appropriate behaviors exhibited by this leader, the senior corporate leadership would see what appeared to be a lack of effectiveness, and the new leader would be replaced by yet another leader in the role. Some of these divisions or regions might go through several iterations of leadership, and perhaps earn a reputation as a market that is typically non-performing or of low potential which discouraged quality leaders from attempting an assignment in a division with such a poor projected outcome.

Both companies were blindsided by the toxicity within them, and unfortunately, this scene is played out each day in various organizations across North America. This can be in any industry and can include nonprofit and volunteer groups. Firms will have consistently under-performing departments or divisions, and both operational and human capital leadership feel powerless to overcome these challenges. They might take steps to address culture and leadership toxicity, but the steps are often fruitless. This is because they don't often know how to break—or even recognize—traditional organizational patterns that encourage toxicity.

This is the first step when addressing a toxic culture. When we can see the traditional patterns that need to be broken, we are less likely to overlook toxicity as the "status quo." We are then less likely to misunderstand the realities of the toxicity within our organizations, and we can take action towards creating sustainable organizational health. This is why the first three chapters of this book are dedicated to helping you recognize these patterns and mindsets, so you can see where the problems truly begin and the extent of them within your organization.

1

SHIFT IN MINDSET

Before we can identify toxic leadership, heal from it, and create a culture that no longer encourages it, we need a shift in the way we think about toxicity—and how to handle it—in the workplace.

When we picture a toxic leader, many of us see someone who is naturally aggressive, abusive, overly direct, or callous. We imagine unreasonable bosses who cancel requested leave or yell at us when we make a mistake. While I can agree these leaders are toxic, and we certainly don't want to allow them in our cultures, they are not the only toxic leaders in the organization. They are only the tip of the iceberg of toxicity.

The reality is that toxic leadership is more about being *self-focused* rather than others-focused.

A self-focused leader might not fit the imagined picture of a toxic leader. In fact, they might have people who really enjoy working with them. Especially because they will often hide their true intentions under the guise of positive values like "family," "trust," and "loyalty." These terms, while seemingly positive, are used to gaslight associates and foster a culture of conformity and quid pro quo, where allegiance is demanded, not earned.

Usually, people don't truly see the toxicity of these leaders until they try to challenge the ideas, authority, or the integrity of the self-interested leader who previously acted as if they were a parent or mentor figure to them. When conducting research, I found that many who participated in the study had experienced this. They often found they were on the good side of the leader until they "crossed" them. Then, the said leader would quickly shift the way they interacted with the associate from positive to negative and would cast them out of the group or even position others against them.

Toxic leaders like this lure associates into a false sense of security. This group then admires their boss until they have a counter idea and are treated like a heretic for it. By then, they are less likely to speak up about the sudden shift in their leader because they see that so many others in the company accept, or even admire, this false-fronting individual.

Unfortunately, this gives no feedback to the organization, and those in charge mistakenly believe that the absence of complaints signifies a healthy environment. This is a dangerous assumption for organizations to make. It overlooks how associates can become enamored with charismatic leaders, irrespective of the leaders' actual intentions. Because of this, they assume no news is good news. But in truth, silence is dissent. When leaders have self-serving intentions, the associates who follow them are often drawn to the allure of being part of their inner circle, which provides a sense of security and inclusion. At the end of the day, we are human, and being part of the inner circle triggers our herd protection mentality. We *need* to be accepted to feel safe, which then reinforces the toxic status quo, making it exceptionally challenging for anyone who questions it to regain their footing within the group.

What's worse, research indicates that susceptible followers often mirror the poor behaviors of their leaders, suggesting that toxicity can proliferate throughout an organization, even if it appears stable from the outside.[3] This dynamic results in an environment where negative actions are tolerated and normalized, significantly undermining organizational performance.

But currently, most organizations don't know how to recognize any of these problems. In fact, many don't realize they have a toxic leader in place until they see high associate turnover. This is where a shift in mindset comes into play. We can no longer use *only* high associate turnover to identify toxicity. There are many individuals who are "reluctant stayers," who may tolerate toxic environments due to constraints like mobility issues, insurance dependency, or other personal circumstances that make changing jobs a risky proposition. We have to start seeing toxicity as more than angry bosses and an obvious lack of empathy.

SCREENING ISN'T ENOUGH

Many organizations try to avoid toxic leaders in interviews. They conduct emotional profiling, personality profiling, and assessments to try and screen out toxic individuals. Yet, these often don't work, leaving the human resources department feeling surprised that toxic individuals slipped through their tests. But the problem is, many toxic professionals can outsmart these tests. Toxic leaders are not monolithic. They come in various forms and can arise in any department or level of an organization. They may not always be the overtly aggressive or visibly undermining individuals; often, they are those who subtly manipulate, coerce, or prioritize personal gains over team or organizational well-being.

Many of these assessments aim to evaluate a candidate's motivations, interests, and leadership styles, yet they often fail to accurately gauge the candidate's underlying intentions. Toxic leaders, who frequently possess above-average intelligence, are adept at understanding and manipulating these tests to present themselves in a favorable light. They can easily align with an organization's objectives if they believe those objectives are in line with what they want to accomplish, and they know the desirable answers. This is particularly true when tests attempt to measure consistency between a candidate's self-perception and how they believe others perceive them. Which means they can easily see through these tests *and* score high on them.

The evolving nature of toxicity presents another significant challenge. Even if initial screenings are effective, they cannot predict how individuals will adapt or change over time. A person who is not toxic at the point of hiring might develop toxic traits later due to various factors, including shifts in personal circumstances or organizational changes. For example, if an organization has lax financial controls, and one of their associates starts to experience significant financial difficulties, they could resort to fraud—not necessarily because they are inherently bad or dishonest, but because the environment facilitates the behavior, and the need shifts their perspective. People are dynamic and go through different stages in their life. An associate's alignment with company goals can dramatically shift when personal or organizational conditions change, creating toxicity due to circumstance.

So, if screening isn't enough, what *can* you do?

Using the Culture Recovery Framework will foster a robust ongoing culture of accountability and transparency that actively discourages toxicity. We will break down how to do this later in the book, but it requires cultivating an environment where toxic behaviors are inherently incompatible with the organization's values and operational norms. By establishing strong systemic safeguards and a culture that continuously reinforces ethical behavior, potential toxic leaders may either reform their behavior to align with the organization's values or naturally find themselves out of place, leading them to exit the organization.

REMOVING TOXICITY ISN'T ENOUGH

I believe it is fair to say that many organizations, once they recognize toxicity, act quickly and often remove that individual altogether. However, simply removing toxic leaders from an organization is not sufficient to heal the underlying issues or repair the damage they have caused. Many organizations are so embarrassed that they had a toxic leader to begin with, that they remove them and sweep the incident under the rug. They do not recognize the conditions that allow that leader to exist in the first place, and they expect the affected teams to get back to business without any time to heal.

How many times has a leader simply disappeared one day? Leaving you and the team happy they are gone, but confused as to what happened? Or, if you are a leader, how much frustration and shame have you felt realizing a toxic leader needed to be removed immediately when you saw how they are affecting other associates at the company? Apologizing in these instances is hard. Making substantial change is harder. It can be difficult to truly identify what allowed that toxic leader to thrive in the first place, and without that identification, it is even more difficult to promise associates it won't happen again.

When toxic leaders operate within an organization, they erode trust and create a work environment that can have long-lasting effects on team dynamics and individual well-being. If a family had a major fire in their home, they couldn't go live in it like nothing happened immediately after the fire was put out. The smell of smoke lingers, burn marks scar the walls, damage remains, and the root cause must be addressed to prevent future fires.

Similarly, removing a toxic leader and immediately going back to business as usual is like expecting your associates to live in a burnt house and ignore the scars. Doing so perpetuates more toxicity and doesn't address the emotional damage left behind. Associates need targeted interventions to recover from the damage inflicted by toxic leaders. This might involve counseling, rebuilding team cohesion, or other supportive measures to restore a healthy work environment on an individual level. But it also includes critically analyzing what part of your culture allowed the toxic leader to thrive in the first place.

Back in the early 2000s, my wife and I owned a martial arts studio. We were fortunate to have worked with the police to offer self-defense scholarships to women who were victims of physical assault. This program provided them with physical defense training and a supportive community to help regain control over their lives. In almost every one of these classes, there was a pivotal point where the women would be paired up with a male from the class. The range of emotions exhibited from them, from breaking down to an over-aggression towards this partner, reflected the PTSD they were still working through from the attack.

Unfortunately, this PTSD exists in associates who have experienced toxic leaders as well. In my doctoral research, I found many instances of medically diagnosed PTSD resulting from exposure to toxic leadership. Associates who have suffered under toxic management will likely display a range of emotional responses, from breakdowns to aggression, reflecting deep-seated trauma. This trauma can't be ignored.

Stephen M.R. Covey, author of *Speed of Trust*, introduced the idea of a "trust tax"[4] relating to how productive a workforce is based on how much they trust their leaders. An organization may remove a toxic leader and replace them with somebody who isn't toxic, but that leader is then often unable to influence and guide the organization and simply doesn't have the trust of the associates they are supposed to lead. This new leader likely didn't *earn* their distrust, but because lingering emotion from the past toxic leader was never addressed by the organization, associates are left wondering if they can (or should) put their faith in the new leader.

Organizations should actively engage in restoring trust and addressing the emotional and psychological impacts on their associates. This involves acknowledging the past issues openly, providing support for affected associates, and implementing systemic changes to prevent similar issues in the future. The Culture Recovery Framework will help you do this. By taking the steps outlined, organizations can steadily restore trust within their workforce.

THE MORAL OBLIGATION TO REPAIR YOUR CULTURE

I have found in academic literature that less than 18% of the research in published studies discusses organizational outcomes.[5] Rather, they simply focus on the toxic leader and how to mitigate or remove them. This isn't unreasonable.

From an academic standpoint, you need to reduce some of your variables, and you can't have too wide of a subject group to study. Further, academic research primarily seeks to understand a set of circumstances, but solving those circumstances is often considered outside the scope of research. However, the reality is that without focusing on the organization as a whole, any removal of toxic leadership likely won't last. As we mentioned before, it isn't enough to remove toxicity; leaders need to find ways to actively move their culture towards accountable and ethical leadership to create value for their associates.

The absence of efforts to add value to associates creates a transactional relationship between leadership and the associates, rather than the dual value of leadership that focuses on developing those within the organization. In an employment or volunteer capacity, the minimal concept of labor or service provided in exchange for a paycheck is outdated, if it was ever relevant. In our contemporary relationships, there is a mutual engagement and expectation that an organization adds value to an individual beyond cash compensation.

At the time of this writing, we have less than a 4% unemployment rate in the United States,[6] yet there is only a 62% overall associate satisfaction rate,[7] with women being the least satisfied, and those that switch jobs being the happiest. The participation levels in employment are high enough to suggest that individuals can go anywhere they want to (or they have multiple job options), which means organizations need to work harder to differentiate themselves. Many HR professionals recognize this and include discussion about how the organization can help you grow in their conversations with potential candidates. They regularly tout great culture, environment, or development provided to help attract top talent. Yet many organizations don't follow through with these promises, leaving the new associates frustrated and disenchanted with the company. And in an effort to warn others, associates use platforms like Glassdoor to reveal the discrepancies and deter potential talent.

During my doctoral research, many individuals shared their observed experiences, including a sense that leaders would turn their head away when bad things happened. Each of the participants shared their belief of how the organization knew of the toxic leadership occurring in the workplace; however, the organization made little or no acknowledgement of its existence, even when it acted directly contrary to the organizational values or goals.

One participant shared: "I see the toxic leader routinely going against what [the organization] says are its priorities, but in terms of their senior leadership, they're just so absent that I don't see whether they're working towards the goals, or not working towards the goal."[8]

Participants spoke often of organizational hypocrisy, which appeared to them to be an allowance, or at least an organizational acceptance of the toxic leader's actions.

Another participant spoke about how their organization publicly presented as a positive environment, where they were promoted as a resource or solution to all [customers];

however, "what I noticed from experience, and witnessed what senior leadership did in reaction to [the toxic leader], it was more like ignoring the model as their actions did not match."[8]

In the absence of addressing toxicity, it was never clear to the remaining associates if the behaviors were accepted or not, and the absence of transparency and accountability reflected poorly on organizational leadership to a significant degree. Trust was breached, and no efforts were made to repair it. Eventually, even those internally in the organization that witnessed this, yet may not have been directly affected, will lose faith in the organization over time.

As discussed in the literature by Thoroughgood et al. (2018), Matos et al. (2018), and Gopinath & Becker (2000), there are tangible and quantifiable consequences from toxic leadership within an organization. These can include increased costs of associate turnover, administrative costs, and legal fees to settle complaints. Less-quantifiable consequences can appear in the form of loss of brand equity, greater difficulty in recruiting, or challenges associated with an internal or inter-department lack of trust.[8]

Leadership in any company has a moral obligation to provide value and repair their cultures so the associates who work with them don't have to experience toxicity. This is how we honor and respect the humans who choose to work for our organizations. Failing to do so creates a breach in credibility and trust both internally and externally.

CHANGE SHOULD BE FELT FROM THE BOTTOM UP

Many organizations initially misinterpreted the mass exit during, and following, the 2020 Covid-19 pandemic as a sign of laziness or an exploitation of government support programs. However, the continuation of high attrition rates, even after the end of such programs, indicate deeper issues. No longer did associates need to tolerate poor or demeaning work cultures, and due to a new understanding of flexibility (such as virtual work and non-standard working hours), we had more options for places to work and were no longer limited to our geographical location in many industries.

This shift gave people opportunities to rewrite how they wanted to engage with employers. Demographically, millennials and subsequent generations expect their employment to be more than just a paycheck. They view it as a two-way exchange where their contributions and well-being are valued as much as their output. This expectation was amplified by the pandemic, which not only challenged traditional work paradigms through shifts to virtual work and flexible hours, but also gave individuals a chance to reconsider what they value most in their employment relationships.

In 2024, Gallup published the findings of their study[9] suggesting that nearly one in every two workers were actively looking at employment options outside of their current role. Further, with a projected 41% of all turnover being preventable, those staying around are becoming more and more disengaged. Initially this was called "quiet-quitting," but now has reached a point where Gallup's designation makes sense: The Great Detachment.

This means organizations need to adapt to the new expectations or get left behind.

Unfortunately for many, this requires significant adjustments to the current norm. For leadership to be effective in this new era, it must move away from "top down" expectations of trading dollars for hours-worked and adopt a bottom-up approach. This doesn't necessarily mean that initiatives must *originate* from the lowest levels of the organization, but the effects should first be felt there. Any cultural changes put in place to discourage toxicity and heal the culture should center on the experiences of these associates first, with adjustments made progressively up the organizational hierarchy to ensure that changes positively impact every level.

CONDUCIVE CONDITIONS FOR TOXICITY

I lived for roughly a decade in the Midwest, and while storms were not uncommon, you had to pay attention to certain conditions that would suggest the severity of the storm. Higher daytime temperatures, higher humidity, and wind moving from particular directions would all suggest the difference between a storm with wind and hail, or a storm that could be a high tornado risk.

While harder to discern in the workplace, there are similar conducive conditions that can result in a toxic culture which then breeds toxic leaders. These conditions, both tangible and intangible, set the stage for negative outcomes by creating environments where toxic behaviors are often inadvertently encouraged.

Conducive conditions for toxicity in an organization can vary widely but typically include factors such as:

- **Overly Competitive Departmental Relationships:** When departments are pitted against each other, the pressure to outperform at any cost can lead to unethical behaviors.
- **Nepotism and Favoritism:** These practices undermine meritocracy, breeding resentment and disillusionment among associates who see no clear path to advancement based on performance.
- **Inaction on Associate Complaints:** Failure to address reports of deviant behavior validates and perpetuates the toxic behavior, damaging trust and morale.
- **Prioritizing Profit over People:** When organizations choose financial gains or client relationships over the well-being of their associates, particularly in retaining leaders known for toxic behaviors, they send a clear message about their values. While a profit motive is a good thing, it is absolutely possible to achieve both profit expectations *and* associate value. It is best when both are achieved simultaneously, as this provides sustainable growth.
- **Policy Inconsistencies:** Different rules for different levels of the organization can foster resentment and a sense of unfairness.

- **Tolerance of Toxic Behaviors:** A lack of public condemnation and corrective action from executive leadership can make toxic behaviors seem acceptable.

Without intervention, these conditions will lead to a persistent culture of toxicity that is difficult to resolve. Some employers might recognize this toxicity in their culture but don't know how to—or don't want to—adjust it. So, they resort to increasing the pay of those they want to keep at the company. But believing that pay is a primary driver suggests a lack of understanding contemporary motivations in the workplace.

Pay began to drop on the priority list when Gen X workers entered the workforce. They preferred pride and a sense of accomplishment[10] over pay. This mindset has become even more prominent as both millennial and Gen Z workers have entered the workforce. Instead of prioritizing pay first, millennials are motivated more by achievement-focused work with consistent work-life balance. And, more so than pay, Gen Z seeks diversity, transparency, and consistent feedback.[11] As leaders, we cannot lean on pay alone to rectify deep-seated issues of toxicity.

To truly shift a culture that breeds toxic leaders, the C-suite should engage in a deep, systemic overhaul that begins with a frank assessment of the organization's current culture and practices. Look at the list above and truthfully ask yourself if any of these conducive conditions exist in your company today. If the answer is yes, it's time to start doing something about it.

REWARD SYSTEMS AND MISALIGNED INCENTIVES

Reward systems and incentives are another condition for toxicity that deserves a deeper review. These conditions drive leadership behaviors and, by extension, the overall health of the organization because they are closely tied to quantifiable outcomes such as company profit, share value increase, or other financial metrics. While effective in motivating leaders to achieve specific goals, these conditions might inadvertently promote behaviors that are misaligned with the long-term health of the organization.

How is this a risk? These incentives can be gamed. For instance, achieving a financial objective by drastically reducing staff might boost short-term profitability but can undermine the organization's stability and morale in the long run. This short-sighted focus on financial KPIs neglects broader considerations that are key for sustainable success, leading to decisions that may achieve quarterly objectives yet jeopardize the organization's future consistency and stability.

Some organizations are beginning to include associate feedback as a measurement tool for executive compensation. This is a good thing! However, this strategy needs to be monitored to avoid misrepresentation. Associate surveys may not always capture genuine sentiments due to the way questions are framed, or because associates might doubt the confidentiality or impact of a survey.

One organization that I worked with recently included in their annual associate survey a question as to whether the associate believed any value would come from the survey itself, and if they believed that their opinion really mattered. Keep in mind, this was a high-performing and value-based nonprofit organization, yet they scored incredibly low on this survey question! In companies where self-focused leaders are in charge, this is typically true, and the associates are likely aware of how little their opinions are considered.

While rethinking reward systems and incentives is a step in the right direction, it requires careful implementation and continuous refinement to ensure that such systems genuinely contribute to a healthier organizational environment. Scrutinize your rewards systems deeply, as they are one of the larger conducive conditions that can lead to toxicity in many organizations.

MITIGATION SHOULDN'T BE ONLY LEFT TO HR

Culture building and toxic culture mitigation efforts are typically owned by human capital leadership and rarely senior organizational leadership, who are more focused on operations and finance.

HR is tasked with talent acquisition, the reduction of attrition, and overall associate satisfaction. It's a tall order. Without the full support of operational leadership, human capital teams are relegated to programs and initiatives that may or may not carry the full buy-in of the operational leadership either in word or modeled-behavior. This disconnect often results in cultural efforts being sidelined, especially in organizations that are driven by quarter-to-quarter performance metrics and are primarily accountable to boards, shareholders, or ownership groups. Since culture-shaping efforts usually require a longer timeline to manifest—often six to eighteen months— they are frequently viewed as supplementary rather than integral to immediate business outcomes.

When HR leaders oversee culture shaping efforts, they usually drive engagement activities based on associate survey findings. A trusted colleague of mine shared with me her belief that "engagement without accountability leads to entitlement." Meaning, without the partnership of operations to both execute and follow up on the accountability expected, HR handling the task of culture shaping will be a one-sided approach that could imbalance the organization.

My conversations with Chief People Officers and Senior HR Leaders suggest that there is a high level of frustration for the lack of operational executive buy-in to the value and support in the execution of these initiatives. This may be because HR leaders fail to make a business case, or, this could be a result of outdated thinking around the transactional nature of associates and the organization. Either way, to effectively address and mitigate toxicity within the workplace, the responsibility should extend beyond human capital departments.

Addressing toxicity requires us to shift several mindsets that are ingrained in the way many of us view the corporate world today. Right now, we feel we have solutions to tackle toxicity. But screening isn't enough, removing toxicity isn't enough, and leaving your culture up to chance isn't enough, because the conducive conditions to create toxicity will outpace your efforts to the contrary. We should do more, and the rest of this book will teach you how.

REFLECTIONS

Understand

1. Recognize toxic leadership can look and feel different in various organizations
2. Accept you may have "reluctant stayers"
3. Remember toxicity provides an allowance for workplace-deviant behaviors
4. Screening alone won't eliminate toxic leaders
5. Removing a toxic leader isn't enough

Act

1. Cultivate a culture where toxicity is inherently incompatible with the organizational values and norms
2. Establish strong and systemic safeguards for the organization
3. Recognize the moral obligation to work towards repairing your culture
4. Address conducive conditions
5. Consider existing incentives and reward systems

2

TOXIC LEADERSHIP

Toxicity is a popular term, and due to its popularity, it has had many definitions—some of which are correct, some which are not. In this chapter, we will analyze the true meaning of toxic leadership, and how to recognize it, so we can start with a clear picture of what *exactly* we want to prevent.

TOXICITY IS PRO-SELF

We discussed earlier that toxic leadership may not always be overtly negative or abusive behavior. Though many of us have experienced this behavior from a leader and know—without a doubt—they are toxic, there are more layers to toxicity that can be difficult to recognize.

A toxic leader is pro-self rather than pro-organization. At first glance, their actions may appear beneficial or even altruistic, but a closer examination reveals that these are often strategic moves designed to further their personal interests. Their charm and seemingly confident leadership style can be incredibly misleading, making it challenging for team members and other stakeholders to see beyond the facade. It is worth noting that some leaders may be unknowingly toxic. They are immature in their understanding of the consequences of their behaviors or may even be oblivious to their own bias towards themselves.

The influence of a toxic leader is significantly amplified by their positional power within the organization. When such a leader holds an influential title and extends praise or accolades, these gestures can carry disproportionate weight. Associates unaware of the leader's true intentions may perceive these accolades as genuine recognition of their efforts, which reinforces the leader's perceived benevolence. However, these praises are often selectively given, aimed at individuals who can further the leader's agenda or given at moments when public acknowledgment serves to enhance the leader's image.

This dynamic creates a particularly dangerous environment because it allows the toxic leader to continue their self-serving behaviors under the guise of effective leadership. The perception of authority that comes with their position makes it difficult for subordinates to question their motives without fearing repercussions. As a result, even disingenuous praise becomes a tool for manipulation, subtly coercing associates into aligning with the leader's agenda under the mistaken belief that they are contributing to a noble cause.

In my consultations with various organizations, including volunteer and ecclesiastical groups, a recurring theme has emerged concerning how senior leadership perceives highly charismatic leaders. These leaders often command admiration and compliance from their teams, which at first glance suggests a high level of effectiveness. Their ability to rally a team and inspire outward enthusiasm can be incredibly appealing to those at the top who are looking for strong leadership to drive the organization forward.

However, this surface-level assessment can be dangerously misleading. Senior leaders often overlook crucial, deeper questions that go beyond immediate team dynamics. One critical oversight is the failure to consider the experiences of individuals who have left the team. What were the reasons behind their departure? Was it a voluntary move toward a better opportunity, or did they feel pushed out by the prevailing leadership style? These questions reveal hidden fractures within the team dynamics that are not immediately apparent.

While compliance and admiration can be indicators of a leader's influence, they do not necessarily correlate positively with genuine respect or effective leadership. Compliance can often be coerced through subtle pressures or the creation of an environment where dissent is quietly stifled rather than openly addressed. Admiration, too, can be shallow, rooted in the leader's charisma rather than their competence or fairness.

This is the type of toxicity we often *feel* before we can put into words, and it is one of the reasons many associates are leaving their positions today in favor of something they hope will be better. In the wake of people leaving, senior leadership must ask themselves what potential contributions might be lost when associates leave. Each departure might represent a missed opportunity to bring new ideas and perspectives to the table that could challenge the status quo and drive innovation.

When a toxic leader is in charge, many who see their toxicity or think differently but know their opinion won't be heard will leave the organization. Those who remain will be those who think the same way as the toxic leader. This fully aligned groupthink can be dangerous in more ways than one. One prominent example was during an airshow rehearsal for the United States Air Force Thunderbirds in 1982. During these shows, demonstration team pilots don't fully look at their instruments. They look at the lead aircraft ahead of them, follow their lead, and keep the required distance between them and the lead pilot, always mimicking the movements of the aircraft they are watching to create their formation. But during this airshow rehearsal, there was a mechanical problem with the lead aircraft. It plummeted towards the ground with all of the pilots following behind. Unfortunately, this entire group of four planes crashed into the ground, with all pilots losing their lives.[12]

While groupthink within your organization may not be this deadly, it will likely hamper the progress of the organization and may even lead to its decline. When intentions are of self-interest, the toxic leader will actively look to terminate or distance innovative thinkers through politics and anti-relational behavior to prevent opinions that might otherwise change their course. Even in environments where intentions are pure, if there is no solicitation of, or tolerance for, different types of thinking, an entire division can likewise "tank" simply because no one has the explicit permission to point out when they are heading for the ground.

TOXICITY INCLUDES SELFISH ALTRUISM

It's not uncommon for organizations to publicly promote a sense of family or loyalty. The goal when promoting "family values" is for associates to feel as if the organization is an easy, welcoming place to work. However, it often means the opposite, and even allows toxic leaders to hide behind altruistic intentions.

The misuse of "family" and "loyalty" by toxic leaders effectively stifles open communication and critical thinking within the organization. It creates a culture of conformity where the status quo is rarely challenged, and innovation is suppressed. Over time, this can lead to significant organizational blind spots, missed opportunities for improvement, and an overall decline in both morale and performance.

On X (formerly Twitter), Adam Grant recently said, "A company isn't a family. Parents don't fire their kids for low performance or furlough them in hard times."[13] The reality of business operations—where decisions sometimes necessitate layoffs or performance-based terminations—

contradicts the unconditional acceptance typically (or ideally) associated with a family unit. Most organizations hope the relation to family will encourage togetherness, mutual agreement, and enthusiasm for the forward and upward direction of the organization. While this concept is admirable, if a leader uses this type of language for their own desired outcomes, it will only serve to break down trust and develop a feeling of hypocrisy.

This risk increases when such familial language is employed as a tool for leaders to achieve specific, self-serving outcomes. For instance, a leader might promote the idea of loyalty and family to discourage dissent or to rally the team behind personal objectives that may not align with the broader goals of the organization. In these cases, the initial sense of unity and shared purpose can quickly give way to feelings of betrayal when associates realize that the familial rhetoric is being used to manipulate rather than to genuinely build a supportive culture.

Have you ever wanted to help your company, and provided feedback to do so, only to be met with an angry leader who feels as if you are personally attacking them? When toxicity rules and an associate dares to challenge the leader's directive, the response is often swift and punitive. Accusations of disloyalty or failing to be a "team player" are levied to silence the dissenting voice and serve as a public example to others who might think to question the leader's decisions.

I worked for a leader who publicly claimed an excitement to work with me because of my diverse background. But, as soon as we started working together, it was clear they had zero interest in any perspective that wasn't a full submission to their mindset. The more time I spent with this individual, the clearer it became that our values and life perspectives were highly different, and this only served to create a greater wedge between us. This leader only sought to surround themselves with subservient loyalists, so any opinions I had contrary to him were ignored or created tension between us.

This can occur peer-to-peer as well. A colleague of mine joined an organization I was working with several years ago, leaving behind a successful role as a global HR leader for a multinational firm. His hiring manager and recruiting team eagerly told him they were excited for the experience and innovation he would bring. But he later told me that after his first meeting with the other leaders in his peer group, a few individuals pulled him aside and told him "not to bring anything to the table that would cause change" because they only had a few years until their retirement, and they didn't want to spend it having to learn new systems or processes. Unfortunately, it was clear these leaders only gave the illusion of wanting innovation, but behind closed doors, their self-interest towards minimal change (and effort) drove their decision-making.

This experience has been common during my consulting as well. I've observed various organizations where altruism has served as a veneer for selfish motives. Altruism in the workplace, when genuine, fosters a culture of generosity and selflessness, contributing to a positive organizational environment. However, selfish altruism is particularly insidious because it mimics the appearance of genuine concern for the welfare of others. While beneficial on the surface, these actions may come with strings attached, expecting loyalty or silence in exchange for favors. Over time, this will erode trust and contribute to a culture of skepticism and cynicism.

TOXICITY BREEDS LOW-TRUST ENVIRONMENTS

When toxicity is present, it erodes trust among team members and between leaders and associates. Individuals who have experienced toxic leadership are often wary of new leaders, withholding the benefit of the doubt that is crucial for effective leadership. This skepticism hampers the new leaders' ability to inspire and guide their teams. And, when an organization fails to address and be accountable for past toxic behaviors, it perpetuates more mistrust, further compounding the trust tax.

This trust tax also manifests through diminished effectiveness in any organizational initiatives, change moments, or culture-shaping measures. When associates question the motives behind leadership actions, it fosters doubt and hesitation for any new incentives. Much like someone walking down the stairs of a dark basement with their hand out in front of them to catch any spider webs or to avoid objects—even superficially positive initiatives are met with doubt and concern because associates don't know if the new initiative will help them or harm them.

Further, this same lack of trust calls into question the intentions of leadership's words and actions. Which leads to an ineffectiveness of organizational goals and contributes to higher associate retention risks because people are more likely to leave an environment where they feel vulnerable and unsupported. Organizations can't stop recognizing toxic behavior, they also have to take steps to rectify the culture that breeds toxicity. Without these efforts, the trust tax will continue to hinder organizational success, leading to stagnation and high turnover.

TOXICITY ENCOURAGES AGENDAS AND VENDETTAS

I once worked with an organization where the toxic leader was obsessed with professionally beating the leader of a local competitor's company. When I investigated further, I found that this rival was previously employed under the toxic leader. Driven by a vendetta, the leader I was consulting for diverted significant organizational resources and focus towards surpassing this other individual's achievements instead of focusing on the needs of their organization. This obsession led to a series of poor business decisions that exposed the company to significant and unnecessary risks.

Though it wasn't something I would have wanted to witness, this vendetta helped me see the leader's broader behavioral patterns towards anyone they perceived as different or disloyal within their company. This leader frequently engaged in semi-private conversations that belittled hardworking, successful individuals who were on the periphery of the leader's inner circle. As a result, these conversations undermined team morale and created an exclusionary and divisive workplace environment.

Toxic leaders often do not operate alone. While they may or may not recognize that they are developing an agenda (a specific action plan or strategy), they rely on the complicity and support of others to enforce their agendas. There is a regular effort to get other people on their side by finding or creating a mutual enemy inside or outside the organization. They achieve this by cultivating an "us versus them" mentality, finding or fabricating a common enemy to rally other associates around.

To susceptible associates, this manipulation will create a sense of belonging, even if the toxic leader has no intentions of reciprocating the relationship. Associates are then drawn into supporting agendas that may go against the organization's best interests or their own ethical judgments.

TOXICITY IS NOT GENDERED

Many individuals try to associate toxicity with gender, and it is politically timely to associate toxic leadership with toxic masculinity. However, the research does not always find this to be the case, outside of the reality of their being typically more males in leadership roles than females. Studies do suggest relationships between male dominance-based offenders and toxic cultures (particularly within a high masculinity contest culture)[14] Yet, my research suggests equal susceptibility with female leaders acting on similarly dominance-based motives. Intentions matter.

I have seen this proof outside of my studies as well as within the clients I've coached. I have a female coaching client who has struggled to gain traction in her professional development and with advancement in her organization. This has not always been the case. Seemingly the only difference between now and at other times is the gender of her supervisor. Her initial leader was male and consistently had a behavior pattern suggesting support and development. Her most recent two leaders were both women who regularly referenced their individual struggles as a woman in the organization, and who demonstrated a need to overcompensate. Surprisingly, they do not demonstrate any of the support and development behaviors they indicated that they needed to the women they themselves lead. Per the client, when challenged on this topic, these women typically acted in a more protective and defensive manner when receiving feedback from other women than from male counterparts or even subordinate male associates.

Toxicity is an individual issue regardless of genders, and it applies to dominance-based status holders.[15]

Dominance-based status holders are individuals whose agenda or feeling of self-worth is typically tied to their role within an organization, their title, or the level of authority they have over others. Rather than a sense of responsibility as a leader, the title itself is the objective, and retaining the title becomes the ongoing effort rather than developing and supporting the team they have stewardship over. Toxicity has to do with people's *intentions*, not their gender. Anyone can become toxic if the culture is in place for them to thrive as such.

TOXIC TACTICS

In my research, I have found that toxicity often is perceived in four ways: manipulation, triangulation, deflection and blame, and responsibility avoidance. The more you know about these four tactics, the more you can identify them and call them out. Remember, recovering from a toxic leader and creating a culture that discourages toxicity require you to produce a culture where toxicity does not thrive easily. But you cannot discourage toxicity if you do not know exactly what it looks like (beyond yelling and belittling).

Let's take a deeper look at each of these four key toxic tactics.

Manipulation

This tactic includes using someone's emotions or ambitions to get what you want. In an offensive effort, this could be using someone's desire to move forward in the organization as a motivator to align with an objective or a relationship that the toxic leader believes will further their own agenda. In a defensive effort, this would include using fear or guilt to keep someone in place.

I recently wanted to hire somebody for a senior leadership role in my firm and found the perfect candidate. They shared with me that they desperately wanted to leave the toxicity in their current environment and were excited for the new role. But, when they resigned, their toxic leader suggested that if they left the organization, they might have to terminate or lay off others due to their departure.

This attempt to guilt the individual into staying unfortunately worked. They stayed with their toxic leader because they feared being the reason others lost their jobs.

Such manipulative behaviors can have *devastating* effects on the workplace, creating an environment where fear and guilt become the primary drivers of associate engagement, rather than genuine commitment or enthusiasm.

Triangulation

In a school yard, triangulation is when child A tells child B what child C said about them. In the workplace, triangulation typically occurs when an individual—often a leader or a team member with influence—deliberately spreads misinformation or shares selective truths between colleagues to foster conflict or mistrust. This may also occur in cultures of low trust and accountability, where non-performing individuals stir up drama to avoid any attention on their poor performance. This includes feigning victimization.

For example, a toxic leader might tell associate A that associate B criticized A's project or performance, even if B's actual comments were either constructive or out of context. The toxic leader's goal is to create and control rifts within the team, diverting attention from their own shortcomings or consolidating their control by positioning themselves as an essential mediator in all communications.

Triangulation can also occur between departments within an organization. A leader might play departments against each other by selectively sharing information to provoke competition or resentment. This not only distracts from larger organizational issues, such as poor leadership or strategic misalignments, but it also erodes the collaborative fabric of the organization, leading to silos and internal competition that can hamper overall performance. This behavior is one of the key reasons that matrix-based organizational structures fail in application.

When triangulation is present, it undermines trust among team members and contributes to a toxic organizational culture where suspicion and paranoia flourish. Teams become less effective as associates are more focused on internal politics rather than collaborating towards common goals. The energy and creativity of associates are diverted from innovation to managing interpersonal conflicts and trying to navigate a manipulative environment without getting abused.

Deflection & Blame

Deflection and blame are common tactics used within organizations to evade personal accountability. These behaviors involve shifting responsibility for failures onto others—whether individuals, departments, or external circumstances.

The most savvy will associate their failures and shortcomings with collectively understood external forces. These factors could range from market fluctuations to supply chain disruptions, when internal mismanagement is the true cause. It is this manipulation of facts that helps toxic leaders maintain a façade of competence and control.

Deflective leaders are particularly skilled at exploiting situations where their superiors are too busy or disengaged to question the excuses presented. In environments where senior leadership is preoccupied with higher-level strategic concerns, or where personal relationships make them reluctant to delve deeper into reported problems, deflectors thrive. They use the complexity of organizational dynamics to their advantage, weaving a narrative that aligns well with understood or plausible external pressures.

This toxic tactic repeatedly undermines the truth, making it challenging for the organization to learn from mistakes or to take corrective actions effectively. It also creates a toxic culture of mistrust, where team members may feel unfairly targeted or scapegoated for issues beyond their control.

Responsibility Avoidance

As an extension of deflection and blame, responsibility avoidance takes shirking responsibility a step further by suggesting there are other higher priorities that should demand leadership's attention. This tactic allows individuals (particularly those in leadership positions) to divert attention from their own responsibilities and failures, dodging the consequences that might otherwise arise from their actions or inactions.

In practice, a toxic leader using responsibility avoidance might consistently prioritize new, urgent projects over ongoing ones that are not performing well, using the former as a justification to shift focus and resources away. By painting these new initiatives as critical to the organization's success, they can conveniently sideline other areas where their direct involvement might be required to address underperformance or errors. This creates a cycle where immediate demands are constantly positioned as distractions from less favorable tasks, effectively burying unresolved issues under a perpetually renewing pile of priorities.

Such behavior stalls organizational progress. It also creates an environment where accountability is diluted. Especially when associates, when seeing this tactic is not punished, may follow suit, adopting a similar approach to their responsibilities. When members see leaders consistently evading accountability and not facing repercussions, it sets a precedent that responsibility is optional.

Keep an eye out for these four toxic tactics. Once you have a clear definition of what they are and how they are typically used, you will start recognizing them. Then, the challenge becomes calling them out. We will address how to do that in Part Two of the book.

With the information in this chapter, you now have clear examples of toxicity, and an understanding of the key tactics used by toxic individuals. This, along with your shift in mindset around toxicity in the workplace, are the first two building blocks you need to break down and rebuild toxic cultures. They are also the foundation for the Culture Recovery Framework and the rest of this book. In Part Two, we will dive deep into the actions required for you to remove toxicity from your organization, and in Part Three, we will discuss how to heal from toxic culture. But first, let's take a closer look at the consequences of allowing toxicity to thrive within your organization. They may be deeper than you realize.

REFLECTIONS

Understand

1. Pro-self = toxicity
2. Intentions matter
3. Toxicity breeds low-trust environments
4. Toxicity encourages agendas
5. Don't mistake family values for actual family

Act

1. Look for unhealthy loyalty
2. Act quickly to disallow manipulation, triangulation, deflection, and avoidance
3. Ask the deep and difficult questions when someone leaves
4. Don't allow the team to crash because they are blindly following a toxic leader
5. Don't make assumptions that someone isn't at risk of toxicity due to demographics or tenure

3

EFFECTS AND CONSEQUENCES
OF TOXIC LEADERSHIP

E ach one of us has seen a toxic leader, or a toxic culture, at one point or another. My goal isn't to suggest that you might not know what this looks or feels like. However, we often know it's *bad* without being able to outline exactly how and why it's bad. Meaning we might struggle to put the negative effects of this toxicity and how it jeopardizes an organization into words, and I'm a big believer that to affect change, you need to understand the reasoning behind why change is needed.

So, for any leader who desires to change the toxicity you see in the workplace or are even working on personal toxic traits yourselves—no shame in that, everyone has something to work on—here are eight key effects and consequences of toxic leadership I have identified through my research and my experience in the field.

1. LOW ASSOCIATE RETENTION RATES

After the great resignation (or perhaps better described as the great reevaluation), associate retention has become a hot topic of public discussion. Studies show that replacing an associate can cost anywhere from 50% to 150% of their annual salary.[16] Despite this, many executives continue to address retention issues with superficial solutions—a strategy which fails to recognize the deeper, systemic problems at play.

Executives often attribute associate departures to isolated incidents, believing that addressing these symptoms will cure the underlying disease. This is yet another place where we *need* a shift in mindset. Instead of blaming these incidents on a single relationship or superficial work conditions, there should first be a larger conversation around the environment in which people work.

Keep in mind that low associate retention rates are not always a sign of a healthy environment. As we mentioned before, your company may have reluctant stayers who remain with an organization due to a lack of better alternatives. They might have to stay because they need access to healthcare or they are geographically limited, or they might be the only one in their household who works so they need a steady income. They would leave if they could, but they can't, and they will often reduce their output and performance to reflect the conditions they are forced to work in.

Gallop recently completed a study[17] showing that the highest engagement with associates was found in fully remote workforces, with hybrid workforces coming in second. Full-time office workforces produced the least engaged associates. On the surface, this appears to be a study showing the value of remote work versus in office work programs. However, digging into the background data and commentary suggests that these workers are more engaged outside the office simply *because they do not have to deal with office politics*, drama, and the other consequences established by in-office work.

Though many senior leaders believe that bringing people in office fosters collaboration, the reality is that they don't organically *create* a healthy space for collaboration unless there is a conscious effort to do so. This leads many associates to believe there isn't any value in coming to the office. Which, if toxicity is rampant within your company, they would be right to believe. If you don't adjust your culture to help workers thrive in and out of office, you will struggle with associate retention and engagement.

For individuals who must stay with a company, either due to a lack of choices or to build their resumes, distancing themselves from office toxicity becomes a survival strategy. The want to move towards remote work is an effort to separate themselves from the toxic culture without actually losing their job. It is a coping mechanism. Those who aren't tied down will quickly leave when they experience a highly toxic workplace, making it harder for the organization to keep good talent.

2. LOW-TRUST ENVIRONMENTS

In *The Speed of Trust* by Stephen M. R. Covey, the author highlights that we use the word trust interchangeably to suggest both moral trust and capability trust.[18] But this is an error in our understanding as these two levels of trust don't always exist together.

For example, I would trust my daughter with my wallet because I trust her to do the right thing, but I would not trust her to reroof my house because she does not have the skills needed to capably do that specific job. This also means that I likely trust my roofer to roof my house because they are capable of doing the job, but that doesn't mean I would trust them with my wallet because I am unsure of their moral standing.

Low-trust environments exist when one or both trusts—moral and capability—are absent. Most leadership practices (especially those in environments where toxicity may exist or thrive if not mitigated) focus on establishing tangible and tactical skills in their workforce that only contribute to capability trust. Unfortunately, these same leadership practices often ignore the need for moral trust.

In low-trust environments, the actions and words of those in leadership and executive positions are frequently questioned, even if not questioned openly. This skepticism stems from unclear motives and leads to resistance towards new initiatives, as well as a lack of candor and effective feedback. When followers doubt the intentions or competencies of their leaders, they become hesitant to fully engage with organizational changes or express their genuine thoughts and concerns. The absence of modeling moral trust and that of holding others accountable further contribute to a disconnect between personal objectives and organizational outcomes.

When trust is lacking, communication breaks down, leading to misunderstandings, misinformation, and a pervasive sense of insecurity among associates. This atmosphere breeds resistance to change and innovation. Decision-making slows as individuals second-guess each other, and collaboration suffers, with team members reluctant to share ideas or feedback. This will significantly slow the company's performance, reputation, and ability to attract and retain top talent, making it difficult to sustain any competitive advantage.

3. LEGAL RISKS

Companies with toxic cultures face broader legal consequences that can have long-lasting impacts on their operations and viability.

When the consequences of toxic leadership and cultures come to light, regulatory scrutiny often increases, leading to more frequent audits, investigations, and heightened compliance requirements, which divert valuable resources away from core business activities. Additionally, a history of legal disputes can result in significantly higher insurance premiums, as insurers view the company as a higher risk. This tarnished reputation can also lead to a loss of business opportunities with potential clients, partners, and investors wary of engaging with a company known for its toxic culture and legal issues.

Associate morale and productivity can also suffer, as ongoing legal battles and a toxic culture demotivate and disengage staff, leading to lower overall performance and a decline in the quality of products or services. Plus, any publicized legal issues or a toxic workplace culture can cause severe reputational damage, eroding customer trust and loyalty and affecting the company's market position and long-term profitability.

These risks can happen in multiple ways, either in terms of legal consequences from the toxic leader on the associate, or legal consequences for the company. Let's look closely at both.

Legal Consequences from the Toxic Leader on the Associate

Working under a toxic leader who stretches the boundaries of acceptable behavior can lead associates to mimic these actions, often without the same breadth of knowledge or perspective. This imitation usually results in associates engaging in behaviors that expose them to legal liabilities. For example, when followers see their leaders engaging in unethical practices, such as misreporting financial data or taking personal financial gains, they might adopt similar behaviors, thinking it is acceptable or expected.

In 2002, Tyco's CEO engaged in significant financial misconduct for personal gain.[19] The company's CFO, acting as a follower, became complicit in these behaviors rather than reporting them to the authorities. The CEO's actions pressured the CFO into manipulating financial reports to meet the CEO's bonus targets. This led to both the CEO and CFO receiving personal financial rewards. However, the fallout was catastrophic: both individuals faced legal action, with the CFO ultimately serving jail time. These events, along with similar contemporary corporate scandals, led to many of the corporate accounting reforms we have today.

More recently, CFOs typically report directly to the board of directors rather than reporting to the CEO. This is because they needed a way to protect CFOs if they were receiving undue pressure from the CEO, as they share numbers with the board that directly affects the CEO's financial incentives. The laws have been changed to protect CFOs from this pressure, but unfortunately, there are many cases where superiors have put pressure on associates to do something unethical that ended up harming the associate's reputation or forced them to face legal consequences.

Legal Consequences for the Organization

Toxic leaders who make decisions based on self-interest can expose the entire organization to legal risks. By extension, these toxic leaders are acting on behalf of an organization, and because of their connection to the organization, their unethical behavior can open the organization to become liable for the consequences of their actions. As an example, when toxic leaders act out against followers and create a hostile work environment, it opens the organization to various legal actions from unlawful termination to discrimination—both of which can be very costly to the organization and ruin its reputation to both customers and future associates.

4. FINANCIAL RISKS

The financial impact of a toxic culture on a business can be staggering, with potential legal fees and settlement costs quickly escalating. According to the Society for Human Resource Management (SHRM), "The top 10 settlements in employment discrimination class actions totaled $597 million in 2022."[20] How much of a dent would that put in your organization's budget?

The loss of trust internally and externally is costly for any organization, and many who have been outed as toxic workplaces struggle to survive.

On top of the legal fees, inappropriate or demonstrated poor behavior can affect brand value, leading to revenue loss, and can dramatically impact share value. A ruined reputation can even make it so preferred suppliers or key vendors no longer want to work with your organization and no longer wish to affiliate with you. Added to this is the cost of replacement, which may include having to pay current and future workers higher wages due to the reduced reputation. These large financial costs incurred could be avoided with intentional culture shaping to discourage toxicity.

5. MASKING COPING MECHANISMS

Coping mechanisms are behaviors or responses due to stressful situations or the deviant behaviors and actions taken against the receiving associate.[21] Toxic leadership often drives associates to develop coping mechanisms that can serve as masks for deeper issues within the organizational culture. While activities branded as mindfulness or wellness initiatives can provide beneficial outlets for managing stress and are not inherently bad, their necessity can reflect underlying toxicity.

Coping mechanisms within a toxic workplace can manifest in various ways. Wellness activities, such as group walks during lunch or yoga sessions, are often encouraged and can genuinely benefit associate health. However, their urgent adoption may also signal an attempt by associates to manage and escape the daily stresses caused by toxic leadership. In some cases, these mechanisms might extend to less constructive behaviors, such as workplace deviance, where associates act out in response to feeling powerless or a loss of control in their professional environment. These behaviors are attempts to regain a sense of control, albeit in ways that may be detrimental to the organization.

While these mechanisms may help individuals manage stress and maintain their mental health, they can simultaneously mask deeper issues and perpetuate a cycle of dysfunction within the workplace.

6. PERPETUAL TOXICITY

When toxicity is removed, but the culture isn't shifted, it leaves a vacuum that is then filled by individuals who assume implicit permission for immoral behavior. Toxic cultures, without recovery efforts, suggest acceptance of toxic behaviors even after toxic leaders are removed. Slowly, but surely—just like "Lord of the Flies"—we will work our way backwards towards toxicity once more. Executive leaders will find toxicity once again exists within their organization, and they will, once again, have to take action to remove it.

Skipping culture recovery efforts is ultimately inviting toxicity; there is no middle ground.

This has been studied and proven in many different scenarios. Social case studies have been conducted where a clean and undamaged car is left on the side of the road for several days and no damage is done to it. But if you break a window and leave that same car on the road, in a matter of days, it is fully vandalized, and everything including the tires are stolen from it. The same applies to an otherwise abandoned, yet well-maintained house that someone sprays graffiti on. In a few days, it will be broken into and ransacked, with nothing left behind.

Why, you might ask? The answer lies in followership principles where permission to act a certain way is implied when an alternative, or preferred behavior, is not expected. These same followership principles apply to a workplace where a toxic leader once existed and the culture hasn't changed. Just changing persons in authority alone doesn't remove the implied permission that poor behavior is tolerated or accepted. Thankfully, anti-toxicity behaviors will have the opposite outcome due to these same principals.

There is a study[22] from the late 70s where nutritionists wanted to research the effects of a high-fat diet. They gave several high-fat foods to rabbits as their test group, and as you might imagine, they had significantly elevated arterial clogging and other associated health conditions. However, half of the control group, for some reason, had 60% less of the arterial buildup and other associated effects.

This stumped scientists, and the focus of the study shifted to identifying what was different about the second half of the control group. The rabbits were the same species and from the same genetic grouping in New Zealand, and there was nothing that suggested any difference that would justify such a dramatic clinical difference. The scientists decided to see if there was something the lab technicians did that may have altered the findings. They ultimately found that one of the lab technicians had a soft spot for bunnies, and while feeding them, would let them out of their cages and pet, hug, and cuddle them. That was the only difference.

They repeated this study twice because it was so compelling and proved how nurture could influence nature.

We learn from these studies that in the absence of a positive environment, removing the toxic leader alone doesn't disallow future deviant behaviors. Similarly, even in environments that are less ideal, when support and trust exist, there is a natural tendency to move towards a positive environment.

If a toxic leader is removed for any reason, but the underlying culture that allowed their toxicity is not addressed, then someone will step up to fill their place because of the implied permission that the behaviors were acceptable, still perpetuating the cycle of toxicity even after the supposed "problem" had been removed. This is also a consequence when executive leaders retain toxic leaders because their performance results are deemed too valuable to risk removing. Profit is a good thing and is necessary for a thriving for-profit organization. Nonprofits and ecclesiastical organizations similarly have their organizational objectives. However, toxicity thrives when high-performing people with bad behavior are valued higher than standard-performing people with good behavior.

To avoid perpetuating toxicity, we need to actively nurture our culture and our efforts to become better. This is where the Culture Recovery Framework comes in, which we will detail more starting in chapter six. Following this framework allows you to introduce an on-purpose, focused effort to continually improve your culture.

7. BUREAUCRACY AND LOW TRUST

If you need something done, do you take additional steps to verify the work output if you don't trust the person who is accomplishing the task? I know I do.

A few years ago, I worked for a company where an old-school mindset pitted sales and operations against each other with the idea that "healthy" competition made everyone better. However, when this created misaligned incentives, where it became possible for one department to win while the other lost, the collaboration and partnership that were essential for success were never achieved because the intentions behind actions were always questioned.

You'll be surprised to hear that this example came from an otherwise high-trust organization. Yet structural orientation and patterned behavior created mistrust, and a bureaucracy developed that negatively affected overall performance. In organizations with specific, identified patterns of untrustworthy actions and behaviors, this issue is magnified. Highly toxic cultures are rife with duplicated work, additional checks and balances, and individuals or departments that choose not to delegate tasks even when it would be appropriate.

The result is that any work accomplished by the organization, whether for-profit or nonprofit, becomes more costly and takes longer to complete. Plus, the increased bureaucracy and low trust degrade associate morale and stifle innovation.

8. PSYCHOLOGICAL HARM AND DOCUMENTED PTSD

In my doctoral research, I found psychologists who believe abusive leader activities could result in long-term consequences such as post-traumatic stress disorder (PTSD). Their behavioral research has shown direct and indirect signs associated with PTSD as a consequence of an associate working for a toxic leader.[23][24][25]

Now, I feel it's important to call out that I don't use the term PTSD lightly. I am fully cognizant of the traumas that most often result in diagnosed PTSD. But in extreme cases, this is an absolutely appropriate description of the consequences of toxic leadership in the workplace. While it hasn't yet been broadly academically studied, The Workforce Institute conducted a survey of 3,400 associates across 10 countries and found that "Managers have just as much of an impact on people's mental health as their spouse (both 69%) — and even more of an impact than their doctor (51%) or therapist (41%)."[26]

Even if not diagnosed to the point of PTSD, it should be recognized that environments that are self-serving to the leader create for others an environment in which they feel judged, discriminated against, ostracized, or experience other mental and emotional consequences of being pushed to the outskirts of the inner circle. This exclusion can lead to significant stress, anxiety, and depression among associates. It is very real, and it is very harmful to anyone who experiences it.

I also recognize there is a segment of the population that may have more of an inclination towards self-serving or otherwise toxic behaviors but are actively trying to suppress or redirect those emotions towards more positive behaviors. They understand these issues and want to address them. But a toxic environment that isn't addressed provides fertile ground for these toxic behaviors to resurface. Just as a recovering alcoholic shouldn't go to a bar, and a recovering gambler shouldn't go to a casino, individuals who are naturally inclined towards self-serving behaviors should not be placed in environments that enable their worst tendencies. Doing so would be a recipe for disaster (or in this case, the creation of a toxic leader). However, individuals with these tendencies *can* thrive in leadership roles when both the organizational culture and the executive leadership expect ethical behavior from them.

Organizations have a moral and ethical obligation to recognize the profound impact of toxicity. They also have a moral and ethical obligation to take proactive steps to create a supportive, inclusive, and healthy work environment. When leaders take this obligation seriously, they can prevent the development of severe psychological conditions in their associates and promote a culture where all associates can thrive and contribute positively to the organization.

NOW YOU KNOW

Toxic leadership is not an isolated issue. It permeates the culture, erodes trust, stifles innovation, and can lead to significant financial and legal repercussions. Remember how the Marvel character Loki said, "I am burdened with glorious knowledge." This now applies to you too. Once you know the exact consequences and effects of toxic leadership, they become difficult to ignore. I won't claim these are all encompassing, but I hope they are compelling enough for you to lean forward and ask how you can stop toxicity from taking root.

Now you might be burdened with knowledge—terribly aware of the consequences of toxicity without understanding how to prevent it—but don't worry, I won't leave you hanging. In the next few chapters, I'll explain practical, research-backed strategies and frameworks to help you avoid toxicity and protect your associates from the consequences outlined in these chapters.

Remember, change begins with awareness. Whether you are working to address toxicity in your current environment or striving to improve your personal leadership approach, recognizing and understanding the far-reaching impacts of toxic leadership is a vital step towards creating a more positive and effective workplace moving forward. Next, let's look at the type of leader we do want to see in our organizations. The *ethical* leader.

REFLECTIONS

Understand

1. We can feel toxicity without necessarily being able to put our finger on the cause
2. Trustworthy environments offer both moral and capability trust
3. Consider if associates seek remote work as a coping mechanism
4. Toxic cultures affect the bottom-line
5. Watch for observed coping mechanisms

Act

1. Model a supportive and influentially positive environment
2. Seek to reach organizational objectives through improving culture, not in opposition to it
3. Fight to eliminate bureaucracy as it masks toxicity and low-trust environments
4. Ensure reporting relationships or general practices don't mask inappropriate influence
5. Don't mistake capability trust for moral trust

4

ETHICAL LEADERSHIP

The ethical leader is the antithesis of the toxic leader, and they are the evolution and maturation of the servant leadership typology.

In its original intent, servant leadership was never meant to absolve leaders of the responsibility to hold their followers accountable. Yet, in many instances, it has done exactly that. Unfortunately, this leadership strategy has been overused and misunderstood. The concept of a servant leader has been mistakenly equated with subservience to those they lead, which has inadvertently removed the element of personal accountability. This misapplication creates a transactional relationship between leaders and associates, where leaders believe their role is merely to serve, without recognizing their duty to foster growth and accountability in their followers.

This isn't an argument against servant leadership. Instead, it's a reflection of what it *means.* In most cases today, the meaning has become skewed, and many people have only adhered to one side of servant leadership—the side that requires them to become a *servant.* Just like Inigo Montoya said in the *Princess Bride*, it makes me want to say, "You keep using that word. I do not think it means what you think it means."[27]

In true servant leadership, leaders have a responsibility to add value to the people around them. While this principle is widely understood and accepted, the practical application often fails to acknowledge the agency of the associate. By removing the agency of the associate, the leader is either ineffective, or by proxy they act on behalf of the associate, which ultimately creates a dependency relationship. This clearly isn't what we want out of leadership, which means that servant leadership is not quite the antithesis of toxic leadership.

This is why evolution and maturation of the concept was required. I first introduced a more formal definition of ethical leadership in a 2022 peer-reviewed journal[28] to provide a more accurate representation of what leaders should strive to be. I defined it as the leadership experience, often characterized and perceived by followers as consistent, fair, and trustworthy. An ethical leader is a leader who is pro-organization and pro-others rather than self-interested.

I evolved the concept of servant leadership into ethical leadership because I needed a clear leadership typology defined for the leader that truly represents the opposite of a toxic leader. Unfortunately, leadership typologies are found in multiple areas of research, from psychology to human capital management to sociology. Yet, no single science agrees upon a refined definition. Because of this, an academic definition was created for the ethical leader to be utilized in future research vernacular.

Ethical leadership embraces the moral obligation to add value to both the organization *and* the individual. They are perceived by their associates as consistent, fair, and honest, and their decisions, though not always popular, are respected because they are seen as genuine and in the best interest of the organization. Their approach requires that associates are developed and held accountable while maintaining and using their agency. By balancing the dual responsibilities of serving and holding others accountable, ethical leaders can truly create an environment where both the organization and its members can thrive.

PRO-ORGANIZATION IS KEY

We discussed in chapter two that toxic leaders are pro-self. Ethical leaders—as the antithesis—are pro-organization. As an example, an ethical leader might decide to implement a restructuring plan that includes reassigning team members to different roles based on their strengths and the organization's strategic goals. While this decision may be unpopular among associates who are comfortable in their current positions or fearful of change, the leader knows that realigning roles will ultimately enhance productivity and innovation. Further, the associates will trust that the leader is making these changes for the good of the organization, and not their own interests.

When making this decision, an ethical leader does not make it lightly and will communicate it transparently. They will outline how the decision prioritizes the organization's needs and the development of its people. The ethical leader will do this because they have a deep commitment to the collective good, even in the face of initial resistance or discomfort.

Remember, ethical leadership can be as much about intent as it is about style. In first responder or military circumstances, some described toxic or even abusive behaviors—like cutting someone off to talk over them or pushing someone out of the way—might be warranted in some situations but may not be inherently toxic. Here, urgency often justifies swift and sometimes harsh direction to be given. However, this says nothing about the intent of the leader. In fact, I would argue that a 911 operator giving strict direction to preserve a life aligns better with ethical leadership than toxic leadership.

Ultimately, ethical leadership is about fostering an environment of trust and integrity. Ethical leaders recognize that their success is intrinsically linked to the success of their associates and the organization. They strive to uplift others, create opportunities for development, and act with genuine intent to benefit the collective rather than their own personal agenda.

POPULARITY ISN'T REQUIRED; TRUST IS

Ethical leaders may not always be the most popular figures within an organization, but they earn deep respect for their consistent dedication to making decisions that best benefit the organization.

Whether in for-profit businesses, nonprofit entities, or ecclesiastical institutions, ethical leaders often face skepticism about their motives or intentions, particularly in environments where trust has been eroded by previous leadership or organizational challenges. As we mentioned before, this is often due to the trust tax left behind by a previous toxic leader.

Over time, however, and through the creation of an accountable and trusting culture, members of the organization begin to recognize and trust the genuine intentions of the ethical leader. Even when their decisions are unpopular or seem unfavorable, ethical leaders are eventually given the benefit of the doubt due to their consistent, fair, and honest leadership style.

Typically, these are leaders that have both influence and position. They can be anywhere in an organization, but they might be identified with low turnover and high associate satisfaction scores. Additionally, these leaders have a track record of developing their team members, often resulting in associates being promoted within the organization or choosing to remain under their leadership despite other opportunities due to the positive and supportive environment they foster.

I recently had an opportunity to spend time with the president of a multi-billion-dollar firm. I spoke at a conference, and he was there to represent his firm and to connect with key industry partners. My previous interactions with this leader suggested that he was very savvy in his business approach. He was willing to make difficult decisions, and when doing so considered both the data and the context. Further, as he interacted with others, I could sense the respect he had earned with his own team and others in his industry.

I wanted to see if this was only my impression, or if there was consistency in his behavior. With some additional investigation, I found that he commanded an authentic loyalty and trust due to his pro-organization focus. No one that I asked believed that he acted on his own behalf, and everyone considered him to be one that found his success through elevating others.

Once the ethical leader has gained trust, they become highly effective in gaining buy-in and support from their team for new initiatives. They seem to have little difficulty overcoming what might otherwise be viewed as a challenging situation such as labor reductions, organizational realignments, or similar shifts in business strategy. Moreover, ethical leaders demonstrate a high level of competency and practical skills relevant to their organization. In high-trust environments, their competency enhances their credibility and reinforces their pro-organizational viewpoint.

Frequently in my workshops and speaking engagements, I discuss the effects of ethical leaders on an organization.

I found that presenting a model of positive leadership can be effective in developing higher leadership standards and expectations in the organization. Ethical leadership, more so than other leadership styles, suggests the statistically greatest significance in affecting millennial retention rates and overall job satisfaction.[29]

Plus, the perception of ethics can add value to the organization through increased retention and lower tolerance for toxic leadership. Research has found a positive statistical relationship exists between the perceived leadership morality and the fairness actions of the leader.[30] While ethical leaders might not always win popularity contests, their effectiveness and positive impact on the organization are undeniable.

3 BEHAVIORS OF AN ETHICAL LEADER

Because the ethical leader is a new leadership concept, and should stand apart from servant leadership, I'd like to offer three key behaviors that align with this leadership's typology: strong communication, collaboration, and ethical work.

Communication

This is less about what is said and more about what is understood. Many individuals believe they are fantastic communicators, yet others struggle to understand what is being said when they speak. Ethical leaders prioritize clear, transparent communication and ensure that their messages are understood as intended. They actively listen, engage in meaningful dialogue, and foster an environment of openness where questions and feedback are encouraged. One of their highest priorities will be to build trust through honest and transparent communication.

Collaboration

In professional and volunteer organizations, we all logically understand that collaboration leads to innovation and efficiency. However, the ethical leader recognizes that it is not in our natural behavior to step away from credit or status to ensure that the best answers and solutions come forward. Ethical leaders model and teach the principles of true collaboration. They encourage team members to share ideas, take risks, and contribute to the group's success, and they do not try to take credit for others' success.

Ethical Work

This commentary is not to suggest that other types of leaders aren't actively working to evolve or grow the organization. However, when the organization feels that the leader works for the benefit of the group, then this is ethical work with its exponential effects. When team members see their leader actively engaged in efforts that benefit the entire organization, it reinforces their trust and respect for the leader. Their visible dedication and hard work inspire others to follow their lead, even if it means facing challenges or making sacrifices.

Look for these three traits. They are key to becoming an ethical leader. If you hope to grow into an ethical leader, practice these three traits with intent. But remember, ethical leadership is more about the behaviors *associates* observe from a leader. You can't call yourself an ethical leader and simply become one—you have to actively work to embody the three traits above.

However, because ethical leadership implies ethical intent, correct behaviors conducted with poor intentions will likely still glean diminished results. If you try to adopt these behaviors for the wrong reasons (perhaps to *appear* as an ethical leader when your intentions are self-serving) you likely won't find success. Desired outcomes may appear initially, but this will be temporary. There is something to be said about human intuition, and even without an individual having poor past experiences that may already reduce blanket trust, as humans, our gut is typically good at detecting falsehoods. We may not always be able to tell if someone is not true in their word, but we can typically see or feel it over time.

IF YOU WANT TO ATTRACT ETHICAL LEADERS

Previously, we talked about how a lack of effort to reduce toxicity in cultures will naturally lead to an increase in toxicity, simply because a lack of efforts to avoid it leaves space for it to exist. As ethical leaders are the opposite of a toxic leader, they gravitate towards cultures that are less hospitable to toxicity. An ethical leader typically has a wider view, is more focused on organizational outcomes, and recognizes their ethical responsibility to help everyone in their stewardship grow. And in organizations that have politics, factions, and self-serving behaviors, they are unable to add value to their teams.

They will likely leave these companies quickly, and sadly, this is yet another factor playing into the current associate retention problem.

In a toxic culture, an ethical leader will feel impotent in their moral obligation to add value to their teams. Especially if they are consistently blocked from helping their teams thrive and unable to help the organization grow by other toxic leaders. This can be difficult to identify or measure; however, digging into commentary during exit surveys might help an organization identify this problem so they can take steps to correct it.

To attract ethical leaders, we have to create ethical cultures. It starts by breaking traditional patterns within our cultures and resetting the bone so we can start building cultures and leadership that will drive our companies towards success. This takes time, patience, and work, but it is possible. By picking up this book you have shown your willingness to make a change. In these next few chapters, I'll show you how.

REFLECTIONS

Understand

1. Ethical Leadership is the evolution of Servant Leadership
2. Popularity isn't required; trust is
3. High trust leads to greater buy-in when change is necessary
4. Collaboration doesn't come naturally
5. Being an ethical leader is about how others perceive you to be

Act

1. Be a leader that actively seeks to add value to each individual around them
2. Communicate and be transparent about your true intentions
3. Recognize that what is said is not always what is understood
4. Teach and model collaboration; give credit freely
5. Attract other ethical leaders by generating a culture that is anti-toxicity

PART
2

PREPARE AND RESET

I n Part One, I introduced you to the regional company which was acquired by the national firm. Here, I'll explain how we prepared to make a significant shift in their culture.

I had developed a connection to both entities. I met their people, I saw the value in the service they provided, and I could align with their organizational objectives. However, despite my own willingness, I did not have sufficient influence in my new role to make meaningful change to the parent company at this time. So, I focused my attention on the newly acquired firm, and hoped that as I worked to help them overcome their challenges, their improvement and growth would add validity to the value of ethical leadership and cultures for the acquiring firm.

As I traveled to the various offices to meet the teams, I found a variety of circumstances were shared by the associate population. As I listened and worked to earn their trust, individuals would point out cases of manipulation and misrepresentation to me. They would share their past experiences of veiled threats and coercion, and how it still affected them and their understanding of their individual potential for growth with the company. I heard stories from individuals that otherwise would have left for other opportunities, but were for some reason limited in their options and felt trapped in a hostile environment.

While I was originally told this was one of the most reputable firms in this specific industry, I was later alerted to the legal ramifications and inherent risks created from actions taken by a few of these toxic leaders, resulting in ongoing lawsuits regarding aspects of culture or behavior and other discovered risks associated with safety and fiscal reporting.

While surprised to find this in an organization so highly regarded, I had seen this before in my consulting efforts. A firm can speak of the larger objectives of opportunities and growth for everyone, family spirit, and similar material for mission statements, then lack the proactive efforts required to avoid toxicity. This organization, like so many others, unintentionally allowed for toxicity by not working to avoid it!

Their goal had been to provide autonomy to leaders, but instead they created a space that lacked accountability. By emphasizing titles and positional authority, rank and tenure were seen as superior to trust and collaboration. And when screening for personalities and cultural fit, hiring managers were allowed to hire like-minded individuals and were never challenged to seek after diversity. Further, no checks and balances existed when leaders desired to terminate individuals who might challenge the status quo. Various popular business and cultural programs were implemented from the top down, but there was little effort to consider the experience of those from the bottom up.

Over the next few years, an effort to recover and reform the organization around trust and accountability commenced. While not yet formalized into the current methodology, the earliest form of the Culture Recovery Framework was implemented. This was not an easy task in such an organization. There was no time to pause the parent-firm's performance expectations while we worked on people and culture. We still had our obligations of customer retention and acquisition, and ultimately to achieve the profit targets we had been given.

While it is true that you can temporarily meet expectations through staff or expense reductions, or you can beat and grind staff to meet retention and growth targets, this simply isn't sustainable nor growth oriented. Assuming a business is already right-sized and conservatively managed, you cannot cut your way to prosperity. For the organization to be healthy, and for us to sustainably meet our objectives year after year, we had to break the old model and put into place something new.

Thankfully there was a compelling story to tell.

This was a many-decade old firm, known for high performance, and they had the statistics to back this up. Though an effort to root-out and remove the offending leaders was necessary, without a different understanding, someone new could step back right into their place. We first had to understand the conditions that allowed for those types of behaviors to flourish. This meant we didn't simply need to review our hiring and evaluation practices, but we also needed to consider the conditions of the team that they would lead.

Was there some inherent susceptibility to follow toxic leaders? Would charisma and gravitas have greater influence than our desired cultural norms and expectations? While we rolled up our sleeves to work, we had to provide a new expectation around what would be acceptable and adopt certain practices that would force difficult conversations so that we could demonstrate accountability and trustworthiness.

It would be a long road, and not everyone would be able to stay along for the journey. The following chapters are some of the mindsets and frameworks we put in place to start down that path.

5

CONDITIONS FOR CULTURE IMPROVEMENT

I once consulted with an organization who had a deeply culture-minded CEO. He was committed to fostering a supportive environment and made substantial investments to ensure that his leaders could participate in workshops, collaborate with consultants, and acquire valuable skills to bring back to their teams.

He talked the talk *and* walked the walk, holding himself to the highest standards and expecting the same from those in his inner circle. His commitment to ethical culture permeated every level of the company. It reached the most junior associates and had a lasting impact on the organization's ethos. He brought this same dedication to all of his previous positions as well, leaving a legacy of strong, ethical cultures in his wake. He was an early example of an ethical leader.

What I found interesting about the effects he had on a culture was the staying power of his influence. When he left the organization, I worried that all the work he put into creating a healthy culture would be lost. However, a former associate who was mentored by him was promoted to CEO, and as a result, the ethical principles and culture the former CEO had instilled continued to thrive through this new leader. The culture had become ethical, and it was no longer tied to a single leader; instead, leaders were shaped by the standards of the culture before they were promoted.

Unfortunately, a time came later when an outside figure became CEO at this organization. They were someone who wasn't enveloped in the previous culture conditions, and this new CEO struggled to maintain the same cultural standards. Many associates were quick to deem him hypocritical and untrustworthy as his inability to achieve consistency, even in operational programs, became glaringly obvious. This leader was quickly replaced by two successive CEOs that were similarly self-interested, and sadly, no later CEO was ultimately able to connect with the people and embody the shared accountability that was expected from the associate population.

Within just a few years, this company was acquired by a larger organization because it was floundering and couldn't stand on its own.

Improving organizational culture involves more than just implementing programs or initiatives, and culture is not a set-it-and-forget-it aspect of an organization. It requires specific conditions to thrive. In these next chapters, I will outline the Culture Recovery Framework, but you'll only find success in implementing that framework if you ensure the right change management conditions are in place. Keep in mind, these are the three conditions I have observed over my time consulting on and studying culture recovery. The companies who have ensured these conditions are present when implementing the Culture Recovery Framework have found success. Those that haven't ended up like the company I described above. Without these conditions, any efforts you put forward to make improvements will likely result in—once more—finding toxic leaders among your ranks.

Conditions for Culture Improvement:

1. Make Change a Unified Organizational Effort
2. Embrace Discomfort
3. Prioritize Accountability (At All Levels)

If you adopt these conditions as you push your culture improvement strategy forward, you'll create a self-perpetuating cycle that can exist in your organization long after you leave it.

1. MAKE CHANGE A UNIFIED ORGANIZATIONAL EFFORT

We have discussed how executive leaders often delegate culture shaping to the human capital team (HR) or third-party consultants. While it's fine for these teams to kick off or facilitate sessions, if the behaviors are not championed and modeled by executive leaders, the efforts will come across as creating status-classes within the organization, which leads to the perception that some people need to follow the rules, while others are above it. This doesn't exactly create a unified team of associates.

In my experience working with organizations, I can often sense the likelihood of the staying power of culture-shaping efforts based on the engagement of executive leadership. When culture shaping and toxic behavior mitigation is delegated, it is not viewed as organizationally important, especially if the HR team is touting something the executive leadership may agree with but doesn't embody themselves. When this happens, any meetings or training the HR team holds will not carry sufficient weight to repair past toxicity or prevent future toxicity.

This is usually most glaringly obvious with how leaders act within these meetings. HR might be upfront in explaining these values and why they are important to the associates, but if a leader is not engaged in the session, it signals to the associates that effort in this area is not truly valued or prioritized. We have all attended these meetings at one point or another. How many times have you seen a leader in the back of the room checking emails instead of paying attention? Or a leader who leaves to handle something of "higher priority?"

For culture to become important to associates, it has to be prioritized by leadership.

In organizations where senior leaders are deeply involved in this process, and equally open to change, introspection, and being challenged by their team, I've seen the most positive adjustments. Successful culture shaping requires a reasonable degree of humility and self-reflection. Further, it requires that leaders take the time in their day to show everyone they prioritize culture with their actions, instead of just their words.

In each of the success stories shared in this book, one defining factor is the executive leadership owned both the *implementation and the results*. They required of themselves anything they expected from their teams. This level of accountability is a key tenet of the Culture Recovery Framework, which I will detail further in chapter seven.

Finally, making change a unified organizational effort means ensuring there are no departments "left behind" on the change. Once one part of the organization adopts culture recovery efforts, they are more likely to recognize any toxicity in their peer-divisions or other departments within the organization. If their behaviors are still accepted, it de-incentivizes other departments to continue the cultural shift. Making the change should be completed beyond HR and beyond any single department. Everyone in the organization, no matter their rank or department, needs to make this change a priority for it to last.

2. EMBRACE DISCOMFORT

Sometimes we need to experience discomfort—temporarily—before we can truly change. Breaking old patterns, and old ways of thinking are uncomfortable processes that our mind and body tend to shy away from. But true cultural improvement won't stick unless we embrace this discomfort.

We will discuss the specifics of how to do this in the following chapters outlining the Culture Recovery Framework, but embracing the discomfort starts with adopting new intentions with new desired outcomes before adopting new practices. This is what ultimately causes people to change how they think. When people think differently, they act differently, and their behaviors shift as a result. Too often, organizations are too metrics focused with an eye on results for the sake of results without realizing that results come from behaviors.

We mentioned earlier that it is technically possible to change results without changing behaviors. This applies specifically in financial-driven metrics; however, these do not lead to sustainable results. If instead we focus on shifting behaviors, we can drive the behaviors that will most likely lead to the desired outcomes. However, when focusing on results, if behaviors alone are considered without understanding context or intentions, then the behaviors may not be sustainable (or certainly may not be trackable) towards the desired outcomes. We have to mature the *entire* conversation to consider the intentions and behaviors that ultimately drive the results we want to see.

We also need to embrace this discomfort consistently for a decent period of time. Every organization will have its own past to overcome. Because organizations may have past issues of trust, either in the organization itself or in leadership, even the best intentions and behaviors will take some time to become perceived as consistent. The trust tax, or other similar lingering consequences of toxicity, will initially act as a lingering anchor, slowing the perception of culture improvement progress.

Culture is not a simple recipe. I can't tell you in black or white terms what you should and shouldn't do to improve every aspect of your culture. When my clients first come to me for culture recovery, they hope my answer will be simple. Do this. Stop doing that. Then everything will be as you want it to be. Unfortunately, toxic culture recovery is never that simple. This process will take time.

Startups or flatter organizations typically can make this kind of change faster. Nonprofits and ecclesiastical-based organizations can also adjust similarly fast, if politics and egos don't act as a counterbalance to the new positive efforts. More mature organizations may take considerably longer, perhaps over a year in length to make significant cultural change, which is yet another place were embracing the discomfort—for a long period of time—is key.

3. PRIORITIZE ACCOUNTABILITY (AT *ALL* LEVELS)

Accountability at all organizational levels is a critical aspect of the Culture Recovery Framework. In preparation for any action, there has to be a comfort level with transparency and candor from the organization leadership about the state of the organization. I have seen the influence of this many times.

Once, in preparation for a speaking engagement, I interviewed a mid-level leader in a company recently purchased by private equity. I asked how they felt their culture had shifted positively. They mentioned that, in their perception, the most widely received benefit was that the new organizational leadership was open and transparent about the current state of the company and about their intentions to improve it. They didn't shift blame to the past or dwell on the negative. The result was an associate population who felt heard and validated by the candor of the new leadership. The fact that they were willing to openly share what they found helped instill faith in the team that the leaders were sincere in their efforts to improve the working environment.

As I said before, one of the primary drivers for a lack of trust is when an organization sweeps issues under the rug or pretends everything is just fine, especially when everyone knows something is wrong *and* knows the issue isn't being acknowledged. Even with the best intentions, sometimes executives don't want to discuss what's going on simply because they don't want to be a downer or shine a light on anything negative. This, with pride or ego to protect—signaling poor intentions—means they may choose not to have this level of organizational accountability. This may be simply because they don't want to appear weak, or perhaps because they are afraid they will lose high caliber talent who may want to jump ship if they believe the business is failing.

Each organization will need to determine what level of exposure is appropriate for their circumstances. But organizational leadership should agree that they need to speak openly and freely about the challenges they see or have been brought to their attention. I'll admit, this is easier said than done. That is why techniques for this will be discussed in the following chapters.

Every time I've consulted with an organization, I have introduced these required conditions for cultural improvement. When they embraced these conditions, they made lasting change. When they didn't embrace these conditions, any change they gained was only temporary. Prioritize these conditions. Memorize them. Bookmark this chapter and review them. Commitment to these conditions within your organization will make the culture recovery journey much easier.

CHANGE BLOCKERS

Now that we know the conditions you need to drive cultural improvement forwards, let's identify some key blockers you should avoid. While I can't give you the all-encompassing blueprint for change, I can give you the primary drivers that typically block change and stop people in the organization from embracing something new.

Here are the five change blockers I have consistently seen companies struggle with:

1. Lack of Leadership Consistency toward the Change

The organization looks to executive leadership for consistency when change starts. Change isn't comfortable, and there may be some resistance to doing things in a new way or with a different approach. If the organization believes a change will simply be abandoned in a few months after their leader's initial intent and motivation wear off, they are less likely to try adopting the new way of thinking.

For example, if a company attempts to implement a new project management system, which the executive team rolls out enthusiastically, but after the initial launch, their involvement wanes, and the associate population can see them ignoring rules they put into place, associates may revert to old practices and ignore the new system. Whether it be a new system or a new policy, associates are quick to notice any lack of follow-through and consistency from leadership. That is why a lack of consistency from leadership toward the change will almost always waste resources and damage trust, making future change initiatives even more difficult to implement.

Before significant change can happen, associates need to know that their leaders will be consistent. This involves not just initial enthusiasm but ongoing reinforcement, active participation, and visible dedication to the new practices. Only then will associates feel secure enough to fully embrace and adopt the new ways of working.

2. Antagonistic Personalities

There may be antagonistic personalities represented by existing toxic leaders or like-minded followers that need to cycle out of the organization before any effective change can occur. Sometimes these individuals cannot be terminated or otherwise forced out initially, especially by a new leader, as it may come across as too aggressive and may even be viewed as hostile or politically motivated. An ethical leader will need to measure what type of change they can implement concerning the departure of toxic personalities before creating issues. Afterall, these leaders might be deeply embedded within the organization and have a host of followers who admire them, which often slows or stops the task of removing the toxic leader.

In my experience, when a new leader actively pursues an ethical culture—even without additional performance management—the toxic players will typically exit on their own within six to twelve months because toxicity is no longer "easy" for them to get away with.

3. Structural Obstacles

In larger and typically multifaceted (or multidivisional) organizations, there may be structural obstacles that will not become obvious until the above obstacles are resolved. This might look like a matrix organization where associates report to more than one leader, or where turf guarding overtly exists. Another example could be when authority and accountability are not aligned, meaning that if accountability for your outcomes is given to a management layer, or to a department, they must also be empowered with the appropriate authority necessary to act. There is little that's more disheartening than being judged on outcomes, yet being required to ask permission from somebody else in every way you work to achieve them.

To executives actively seeking to create and foster an ethical culture, the process of resolving one change blocker, only to find another, may be disheartening as well. It's like peeling layers from a head of lettuce, hoping to find fresher leaves within, only to continue finding layers that need to be addressed. This process takes time, patience, and consistent effort. You will face uncomfortable conversations, gaslighting, and frustration when peeling back these layers. But removing toxic leaders from your organization and moving towards a healthier culture is worth the pain.

4. Superficial Engagement Efforts

Organizations often fall into the trap of believing that superficial engagement efforts can drive meaningful change. Conducting annual associate satisfaction surveys, implementing bonus plans tied to these scores, and rolling out action plans to address the most glaring issues are frequent practices. Survey questions like "Do you feel valued in the company?" or "Would you recommend a friend to work here?" are common and well-intentioned, but they often miss the mark because the primary goal becomes improving a score rather than genuinely transforming the associate experience.

Unfortunately, in corporate acquisitions and private equity business turnaround efforts, it's not uncommon to make temporary changes to boost short-term financial performance. Reducing staff, cutting costs—these actions can temporarily improve profitability margins and make the company look good to shareholders or potential buyers, but these are not sustainable strategies. Similarly, in people initiatives, scores can look good temporarily through compensation and recognition programs, but without genuine intent, these efforts won't lead to a better workplace.

Having a "Best Place to Work" certification is valuable, but unfortunately, many aren't earning this certification for their staff—rather, want it as a marketing differentiator. Stop superficial engagement efforts. Instead, every effort should be rooted in a genuine desire to support and develop our people, creating lasting, meaningful improvements that genuinely enhance the associate experience.

5. Lack of Collaboration

It would be difficult to find a people leader who did not logically understand and believe there is a high value in organizational collaboration. Whether that collaboration be within a small team, or department-to-department, it is a goal that most everyone wants to achieve. However, most people leaders do not know how to foster collaboration, nor do they know how to model collaborative behaviors. This is not a skill taught in business school, and in fact, it's often only taught by a small number of authors and consultants. This book isn't intended to teach collaboration, but in the corporate world we often expect collaboration as an outcome while we don't effectively equip or train our teams and leaders towards this end.

Typically, a collaborative environment is one where collaboration is the norm rather than a programmatic exception. It starts as a purposeful exercise (which may be awkward and clunky in the beginning), and with repeated and consistent application, it becomes self-replicating. Culture recovery cannot happen if the associate population, and its leadership, don't understand how to collaborate.

Do everything you can to avoid the five change blockers above. As soon as you spot them, call them out and make it known that they are not welcome. You may need to do this more at the beginning of your cultural shift but keeping these top of mind and addressing them quickly will help make your culture recovery efforts last beyond a single leader.

A SIDE NOTE: GREATER COST DOES NOT EQUAL GREATER IMPROVEMENT

I have been employed by, or consulted with, many organizations that spent perhaps hundreds of thousands of dollars on programs and initiatives with myself and others. These can include speakers, books, workshops, consultants, and perhaps even calendared meetings to instill terminology and process with the hopes of improving culture and reducing toxicity. I certainly do not fault the intention. However, so many of these organizations do this with some flawed belief that this alone changes an organization. The belief that if we only added this one new piece of technology, or made this one organizational change, and everything would be fixed, is like shuffling a deck of cards and expecting the quantity of cards to change. It simply won't make a difference.

Culture improvement doesn't necessitate major expenses or programs. It requires a willingness to change. As a consultant and an author myself, I certainly don't want to suggest that our contribution is not valuable or worth the investment of time and money! But, I often tell my clients that they cannot expect that my time and effort alone in consulting or training their leaders will be enough. I can't steer a parked car. There is nothing I can say in the limited time I have with an organization that can account for every circumstance and situation. And certainly more, there is nothing I can say that becomes somehow more powerful than an apathetic and disengaged executive team.

It is appropriate for an organization to engage outside support, such as consultants, facilitators, or even a programmatic approach to culture change, and the money spent on this effort is typically worth the cost. However, if the *adoption* and *application* of the principles are not visible from the most senior executive team, and all individuals in leadership capacity are accountable to maintaining those standards, then any investment made will have diminished returns.

Executive leaders need to commit to maintaining their course of action, consistently demonstrating the desired behaviors, and holding themselves to the same standards as everyone else before making any investments. If their willingness to change is present, they can expect significant positive results, rather than just a superficial improvement from new buzzwords and costly programs.

Now, with the conditions for culture improvement in mind, let me introduce you to the tried and proven Culture Recovery Framework.

REFLECTIONS

Understand

1. Organizational culture is never set-it and forget-it
2. Executive engagement is a leading indicator for the success of culture-shaping efforts
3. Discomfort comes before change
4. When people think differently, they act differently; results come from behaviors
5. The organization see the challenges, even if you don't acknowledge them

Act

1. Talk the talk *and* walk the walk
2. Make change a unified organizational effort
3. Embrace discomfort
4. Prioritize accountability at all levels
5. If you want to change results, focus on changing behavior

6

CULTURE RECOVERY FRAMEWORK— ORGANIZATIONAL ACCOUNTABILITY

N ow—finally—we can address how to fix toxic cultures. I developed this framework as a pathway to help organizations recover from and prevent toxic leadership. It is a scientifically derived tool that creates a path for organizations to re-develop trust in the organizational leadership, and it represents a pattern of behaviors designed to affect and influence accountability and trust in both leadership and associates.

To be clear, this is not an academic philosophy. I have put it to the test both in my research—which has been peer-reviewed and published—and in my consulting across multiple organizations. It works proactively and enables organizational leadership to cultivate a culture that repels toxicity and reduces the risk of workplace deviant behaviors. But what's more, it is a simple tool that is applicable to all organizations, including volunteer, nonprofit, and ecclesiastical groups which is rooted in the scientific principles of business, psychology, sociology, and human capital management.

When applied fully *and* consistently, this tool produces lasting effects, enhancing associate retention without degrading organizational performance. When you use it, you'll find that associate retention does not have to require compromising workplace expectations. Rather, you will develop a culture of trust and accountability that is inherently magnetic towards ethical leaders and repels toxic leaders and their associated cultures.

On the next page, I've included an image of the Culture Recovery Framework. You'll see it consists of four key quadrants, each representing behaviors that reflect specific mindsets and intentions. While the work associated with all quadrants is simultaneous, you will likely find the best results by progressing clockwise *around* the framework, beginning with organizational accountability.

This chapter will focus on the organizational accountability quadrant of the framework. We start with accountability, as my research shows that associates are willing to forgive leadership for past toxic behaviors *if* the current leaders are open and acknowledge the discrepancy between the toxic leader's actions and the organization's stated vision

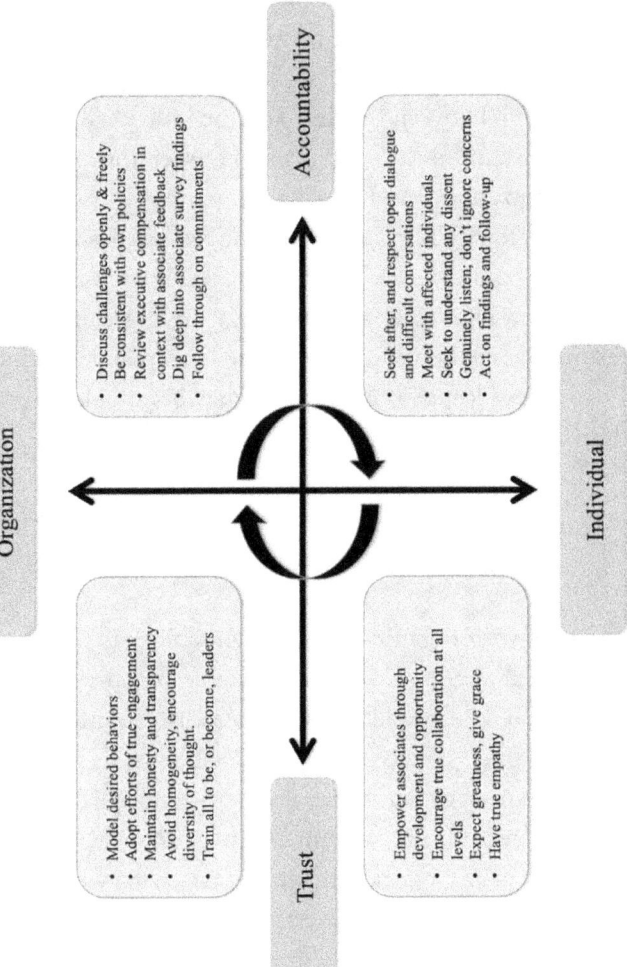

Accountability

- Discuss challenges openly & freely
- Be consistent with own policies
- Review executive compensation in context with associate feedback
- Dig deep into associate survey findings
- Follow through on commitments

- Seek after, and respect open dialogue and difficult conversations
- Meet with affected individuals
- Seek to understand any dissent
- Genuinely listen; don't ignore concerns
- Act on findings and follow-up

Organization

Individual

- Model desired behaviors
- Adopt efforts of true engagement
- Maintain honesty and transparency
- Avoid homogeneity, encourage diversity of thought.
- Train all to be, or become, leaders

- Empower associates through development and opportunity
- Encourage true collaboration at all levels
- Expect greatness, give grace
- Have true empathy

Trust

and mission. This organizational integrity involves those in leadership roles to demonstrate humility, ownership, and self-awareness so they can recognize the breach in trust and take responsibility for addressing it. While trust (pertaining to the second half of the framework) refers to the relationship between the firm and the individual, accountability pertains to the relationship between the leaders and the organization.

The accountability between these two parties is built on both sides of the fence. That is why organizational accountability *and* individual accountability are both required to restore the relationship between leadership and associates. Let's take a deeper look at what behaviors should be practiced within the first quadrant.

ORGANIZATIONAL ACCOUNTABILITY

The goal with organizational accountability is to demonstrate that leadership is accountable to the associate population. Unfortunately, this often runs counter to typical workplace culture, where leadership tends to exhibit behaviors suggesting some level of accomplishment or elitism. Instead, an accountability culture suggests the inversion of the typical organizational chart, where those at the "top" carry the greatest responsibility of service to the organization.

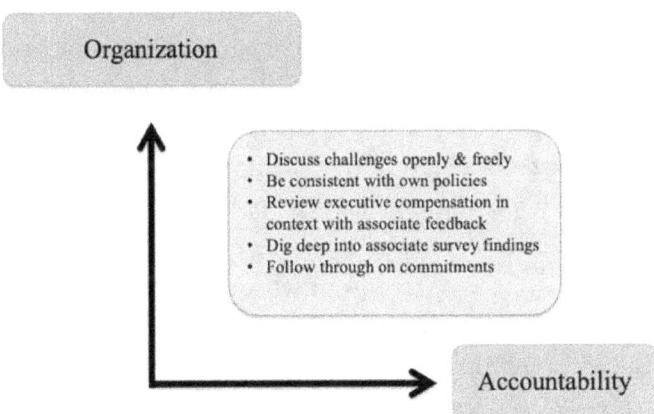

The core of organizational accountability lies in fostering a culture where leaders are seen as stewards rather than *rulers.*

The specific five points in this quadrant of the framework may not apply in every organization and in every circumstance—especially if you are a nonprofit or volunteer organization. However, the principles still apply, including those around compensation and direct solicitation of feedback on leadership performance from the associate population.

1. Discuss Challenges Openly and Freely

Many leaders may resist airing "dirty laundry" because they fear it will diminish their status, ego, or outward appearance. Others hesitate to discuss challenges because they worry it might create a perception that there are significant issues within the organization or demotivate the team. But open and honest discussions about challenges are required for building a culture of accountability—especially because a lack of transparency is often more damaging and usually leads to poor associate retention or engagement because it may come across as an inability or unwillingness to recognize the reality of the situation.

Make it a goal to create a safe space to share challenges openly and to encourage inclusive problem solving. You can even make it a part of your schedule to provide regular updates on the status of any issues or challenges to keep associates informed and engaged in the problem-solving process.

Remember, associates are usually aware of the issues within the organization. Afterall, no organization is truly "perfect." What associates need is confirmation that leadership is *also* aware of these issues and is taking steps to address these challenges. When leaders openly discuss the problems and hurdles the organization faces, it shows that they are aware and committed to finding solutions.

2. Be Accountable to Your Own Policies

Being accountable to your own policies sounds straightforward, but it can be surprisingly challenging in practice. This principle extends to both obvious and subtle situations within an organization. If there are expectations at the lowest levels of the organization, such as punctuality, updating reports, or adhering to accountability measures, then senior leadership should not operate under a different set of rules.

Now, I do understand that most senior leadership roles tend to be results-oriented instead of process-oriented. But, even when this is the case, the fundamental principle remains: if a leader commits to something, they need to follow through. If unforeseen obstacles arise, they should candidly communicate the status and challenges. This shows the associate population that the leader is accountable to their own policies, which in turn pushes the associate population to take accountability seriously within their own roles.

As part of this, we also need to remember that optics matter. Leaders need to actively work to eliminate any perception that there is a different set of rules for different people within the organization. In the book *It's Your Ship*, Captain D. Michael Abrashoff[31] wrote about navy culture, where officers would cut the chow line to get their food ahead of the enlisted crew. Rather than telling his officer group that they were taking advantage of their position, he simply went to the back of the line. Though nearly everybody in the line tried to get him to move up to the front, he refused, simply saying "Leaders eat last." Within a short period of time, his leadership team got the message, and every other leader started at the back of the line as well. This was one of many steps he took to move his ship from the lowest to the highest ranked operational vessel in the pacific fleet.

Do executives have parking spaces that are closer? Are there expectations on some levels of the organization that upper organizational levels believe are beneath them? While the examples given here are seemingly simple or superficial, they have a big influence on the optics of accountability. Ask yourself, inside your own organization, do you adhere to all your policies? For example, if you have an escalation path prescribed for any type of troubleshooting, do you follow that path, or do you simply go directly to the department head, getting what you want and effectively "skipping" the line others are expected to follow? How do you think other associates view this privilege? I can tell you now, the optics aren't good. Especially if you give off the air of "I'm more important and busier, so I get to go to the front of the queue." No matter what level of busyness you experience, taking special benefits or ignoring your own policies gives permission for associates to shirk accountability within their own roles.

I travel extensively for my work and often receive free upgrades to first class due to my high rewards status with an airline. However, if I'm traveling with colleagues from my organization, I decline these upgrades to avoid any perception of favoritism or privilege. Similarly, when renting vehicles, I choose more modest models to avoid the optics of pulling up in a luxury vehicle while my team adheres to a more modest travel policy. It's not that I'm violating any rules, but I certainly don't think that someone from my team will stop and ask me if it was a free upgrade. The risk is that they will assume I received some greater privilege than they did because I am the leader, and that isn't something I want others to feel or assume.

Similarly, I was recently working with an organization that made proactive expense reductions which resulted in staff layoffs. After facilitating a performance coaching and accountability workshop with the executive team, we had plans to have a group dinner with some of the senior executives. The original reservations were for a popular steakhouse, and I felt compelled to recommend to the firm president a more modest evening. Not because every business meeting needs to be at an establishment with a drive through, but because they hadn't thought of the optics. How would it be perceived by the organization if someone happened to see the same group that had laid off some of their coworkers now having a high-cost meal at company expense?

When we as leaders hold ourselves to the same standards we expect from our associates, we demonstrate genuine accountability and foster a culture of trust and respect. This consistency will strengthen the organizational culture and ensure that every member feels they are treated fairly.

3. Review Executive Compensation in Context with Associate Feedback

There is a growing movement towards a triple bottom line approach, where senior executives are judged on their performance across three metrics: profit, people, and planet. While this concept is gaining popularity, it remains relatively limited to Chief Executives and their compensation relationships with the board of directors. Metrics associated with people often include superficial measures such as year-over-year reductions in turnover or associate survey scores. As mentioned in previous chapters, these metrics cannot only be gamed, but they also may not represent true associate opinions, especially when you consider other contributing factors as to why people may "stick around" despite any adverse culture.

It is beyond the scope of this writing to prescribe how boards and compensation committees should structure total rewards. However, it is reasonable to advocate for a significant effort in reviewing executive compensation in conjunction with associate feedback. Various circumstances may cause a dip in traditional associate metrics. For instance, a decrease might reflect the departure of toxic leaders or typical reactions to organizational changes. In such cases, associate feedback should be reviewed in context, recognizing that these shifts could indicate positive changes driven by leadership's pro-organizational behaviors.

Reviewing executive compensation in this context ensures that leaders are held accountable for financial performance *and* for the well-being of their associates.

4. Dig Deep into Associate Survey Findings

While this was discussed at length in previous chapters, I want to reiterate that thoroughly analyzing these surveys shows that leadership is actively listening and committed to improvement. By delving into the details of associate feedback, leadership can identify underlying issues that might not be immediately apparent from surface-level data. Moreover, it shows associates that their opinions are valued and that leadership is willing to take concrete actions based on their input.

This behavior not only addresses immediate concerns but also builds a culture of continuous improvement and mutual respect. Associates are more likely to engage and contribute positively when they see their feedback leading to tangible changes. In turn, this boosts morale, enhances trust, and ultimately drives better organizational performance. Empathy is a critical component in ethical leadership, and by using associate feedback to guide decisions and actions, leaders can show a genuine understanding and concern for their team's well-being.

5. Follow Through on Commitments

While this may seem inherently obvious, this can actually be one of the more difficult aspects of the application of organizational accountability. Leaders are often inundated with numerous initiatives, programs, and ideas, many of which come from the field. However, in the broader business or nonprofit operational context, it's impossible to implement *every* good idea. This reality inevitably leads to broken commitments.

The expectation is not to fulfill every single commitment, but rather to ensure transparency and communication when commitments cannot be met. When a commitment cannot be honored, the affected associates should hear it directly from the leader who made the commitment, instead of relying on a letter or a mass email. The ethical leader should personally reach out, whether by phone, video call, or in-person meeting. This way, they can look that team member in the eye, recognize the commitment was important to them, and offer an explanation as to why it is not something that can be done at this point in time.

This isn't about educating someone on the business matters behind the scenes or checking a box on a to-do list, but rather making a human connection where you as a leader recognize that your commitment to that person may be even more important than the results of that commitment in the first place.

Once you move through these five steps within the organizational accountability segment, you can move to individual accountability. When organizational accountability is exhibited consistently, it naturally leads to individual accountability.

REFLECTIONS

Understand

1. The Culture Recovery Framework works only when applied fully *and* consistently
2. Associate retention does not mean you need to compromise workplace standards of performance
3. Associates will forgive if leadership is open and honest about the past challenges with the toxic leader(s)
4. Don't be afraid to speak of the organization's shortcomings; don't dwell on the negative, but don't ignore it either
5. Optics matter

Act

1. Discuss challenges open and freely
2. Be accountable to your own policies
3. Review executive compensation in context with associate feedback
4. Dig deep into associate survey findings
5. Follow through on commitments

7

CULTURE RECOVERY FRAMEWORK—INDIVIDUAL ACCOUNTABILITY

Accountability can certainly be practiced on an individual level, but without organizational accountability, it remains largely transactional, benefiting the individual leader rather than the organization. However, when organizational accountability is established, individual accountability gains far greater significance and impact. This interdependence is true for all quadrants of the Culture Recovery Framework.

Individuals will not consistently feel accountable to the organization until they perceive that the organization is accountable to them. I do recognize that this is counterintuitive to traditional employer power dynamics which look at the associates as resources for which the organization pays for. In a contemporary model, the associate has an expectation that the trust and accountability they exhibit to the organization should be earned by the organization rather than demanded in exchange for a paycheck. When an individual sees the organization is accountable to them, it provides a moral foundation by which the organization can expect accountability from the individual associate.

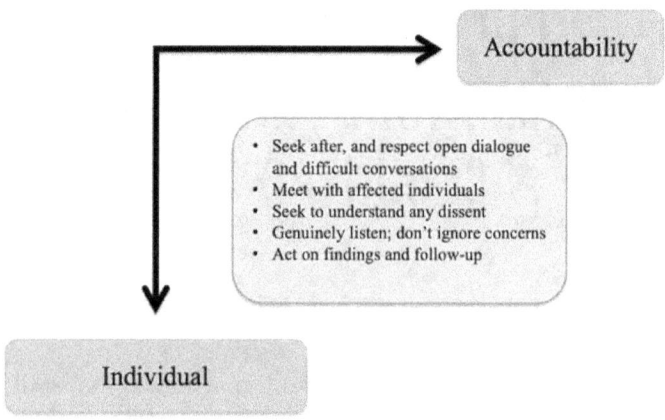

You can see, based on this description of individual accountability, why it relies so heavily on creating organizational accountability first. However, once organizational accountability is established, you can follow these five steps to continue to foster individual accountability within your organization.

1. Seek After and Respect Open Dialogue and Difficult Conversations

Many associates have been socially conditioned to avoid complaining or expressing vulnerability. Consequently, they often lack an outlet to feel heard, acknowledged, or to have their concerns noted. This creates a situation where the larger organization consequently misses out on crucial feedback that could reveal deficiencies or toxicity within the culture. When they do express any feedback they might have, they may do so in an aggressive or semi-offensive manner, simply because these emotions have been bottled up for so long, or they don't know how to best express their feedback.

It is the ethical leader's responsibility to proactively engage with associates and facilitate these conversations. Liz Wisman in her book *Multipliers*,[32] said that multipliers "liberate people from the oppressive forces within corporate hierarchy." I recognize this is not an easy task, especially when balancing client engagement, new business initiatives, and financial reporting. However, failing to create opportunities for these conversations, even if unintentionally, reflects a perceived lack of interest from organizational leadership.

As challenging as it may be to avoid becoming defensive or pointing out an associate's deficiencies, the goal of this step is to listen and authentically understand their perspective. Correction and guidance can come later.

In the book *The Way to Coach* by Andrew Neitlich,[33] he said, "Coaching without permission is simply nagging." You have to give your associates this permission to share criticisms, otherwise they won't feel that their words are allowed or welcome; and when they do offer upward coaching, they will likely feel as if they are doing something that could hurt their career. However, if you are open, and give implicit and blanketed permission, making it clear that you are continually seeking feedback, you can create a lasting open dialogue for potentially difficult conversations.

2. Meet with Affected Individuals

Beyond the removal of a toxic leader, there is also the necessity to help those who may view themselves as a victim of the toxic behaviors of the now departed leader.

As mentioned previously, many executive leaders act as if there are no lingering effects of the toxic leader after they have left. This only breeds more hurt and mistrust among associates. It is our moral obligation as leaders to acknowledge the pain caused. Addressing these affected individuals may not require much more than simply listening and showing empathy. However, the absence of such efforts suggests a lack of care or awareness on the part of executive leaders.

Unfortunately, if these conversations do happen, they are often left for HR professionals. While HR's involvement is not bad, affected associates also need to hear directly from executive leaders. Without direct communication from those in charge, the affected associates will likely create a narrative that suggests the toxic leader's behaviors were tolerated or accepted and that their pain is not taken seriously. A simple, empathetic conversation with an ethical leader can reinforce the genuineness of the organization's commitment to disavowing former toxic behaviors and restoring a healthy workplace culture.

3. SEEK TO UNDERSTAND DISSENT

One of the most challenging aspects of individual accountability is seeking to understand dissent. Similar to fostering open dialogue, ethical leaders must be prepared to receive and process concerns from associates, even when they are delivered in ways that may seem whiny, entitled, or judgmental. Ethical leaders filter out the delivery style, avoid taking offense, and focus on understanding the core concerns and their impact on the associate.

Silence can also represent dissent, especially in low-trust organizational cultures or in the wake of toxic leadership. Due to receiving negative consequences in the past, associates may not feel a sense of "contributor or challenger safety," as outlined in Tim Clark's book *The 4 Stages of Psychological Safety: Defining the Path to Inclusion and Innovation*.[34] This silence, however, is a quick way for leadership to miss out on good ideas.

Reaching out to someone exhibiting silent dissent can quickly establish a genuine connection and build trust. However, dissent doesn't always equate to truth. Remember, this process isn't about accepting everything at face value and making changes to counter every concern.

Instead, it's about ensuring that those who disagree with a position or have a different impression of circumstances have an opportunity to be heard by someone genuinely seeking to understand.

4. Genuinely Listen; Don't Ignore Concerns

I recently spoke with a mid-grade level contributor who was a high performing individual. Her role was new to this company, and her director was a new people-leader who stacked on more work than could be reasonably managed by this particular role.

When I asked the individual contributor what transpired in her conversations with her director, she shared that she respectfully said her plate was full. The director's response was to "Get to it when she could." Superficially, this may sound polite, but in truth, it's almost passive aggressive. The director is still indicating that she has an expectation that this person should still do the work, even if she is lenient in the time frame, which doesn't remove the stress off the individual contributor who already feels they are overwhelmed.

The director, unaware that she was assigning 150% of the workload typical for this position in other firms, failed to recognize or address the underlying issue. The individual contributor felt dismissed, believing that her concerns were merely waved off, and the director moved on to the next task on her list.

This story is unfortunately a common occurrence where leaders believe they already understand or don't feel they have the time to dig and gain a full understanding of the actual problem. This becomes particularly dangerous when concerns involve red flags of toxicity or unethical behavior within the organization. In my experience working with organizations who are trying to recover from toxicity, a frequent refrain is, "I told them about their behavior." Yet, even though they were alerted to the toxicity, leaders overlooked these critical concerns, leading to unresolved issues which eventually escalated into a culture brimming with toxicity.

It's important to note that not every concern will result in the desired outcome for the individual. The goal isn't to fix everything, but to ensure that individuals feel heard and valued. By actively listening, leaders can get a clearer understanding of toxicity that might be occurring, adjust where possible, and reassure associates of their worth both as people and as valuable contributors to the organization.

5. Act on Findings and Follow Up

In the South, there's a saying: "Says easy, does hard." While something might seem simple when you talk about it, it is often difficult to do in practice.

After engaging in interpersonal interactions, you might find yourself with a list of desired changes or adjustments that seem necessary for improving the organization. However, you may quickly discover that there are not the resources, or maybe even the will, by others in authority to make those adjustments. There may be many things you'd like to do for these affected individuals but simply can't because certain processes or permissions are entirely out of your control. Or, associates might request unreasonable or unattainable changes or restitution which may not reflect the realities of organizational limitations.

Do what you can but acknowledge what you can't. This step is more about communication than necessarily "fixing" everything. I've seen many organizations conduct listening sessions or similar opportunities for associates to express concerns. Often, only one or two very public changes are made, and everything else seems to be discarded, which leads to a perception that the organization doesn't truly care.

Follow up is about revisiting the concerns shared by the individual(s) and being transparent about what can and cannot be done to resolve the issue. Even if a concern cannot be fully rectified, it may simply be enough to come back and tell the individuals that they were heard, and that the organization will continue to look for opportunities to improve in that area. However, this response is best given after some time has passed. If this is said at the time the concern was shared, the response will be received as scripted and superficial, so be wary of automatically responding this way, especially if the associate can clearly see you haven't spoken to any other leaders about their concern. If the concern is revisited at a later date with the associate, it will likely show your genuine care for the issue and help to stimulate trust as well as a sense of duty to the organization.

ACCOUNTABILITY FINAL THOUGHTS

You will likely note that all these recommended actions are roles and responsibilities of leaders within the organization. Even when speaking of individual accountability, you may wonder "What do the associates need to do?"

Remember, associate roles are defined by their job descriptions or their volunteer charter. An organizational leader cannot expect individuals to work towards organizational objectives when a culture exists that is counterproductive to those outcomes. What *we*—those of us reading this book—need to do is become ethical leaders who are looking to build and support a culture that removes toxicity and encourages individual behaviors that support and align with our desired organizational outcomes.

REFLECTIONS

Understand

1. Associates will not feel accountable to the organization, until they first perceive that the organization is accountable to them

2. Associate accountability can no longer be demanded in (only) exchange for a paycheck

3. A simple, empathetic conversation with an ethical leader can reinforce the authenticity of the organization's commitment to disavowing former toxic behaviors and restoring a healthy workplace culture
4. Acknowledging concerns is about communication, rather than trying to fix everything

Act

1. Seek after and respect open dialogue
2. Meeting with all affected individuals
3. Seek to understand any dissent
4. Genuinely listen and don't ignore concerns
5. Act on findings and follow up

8

CULTURE RECOVERY
FRAMEWORK—
INDIVIDUAL TRUST

E arlier, we defined toxic leadership as pro-self leadership, which stands in direct opposition to what associates expect. Followers believe that in exchange for their efforts, leaders should provide productive feedback, guidance for improvement, and opportunities for growth. But when trust is absent, followers start to feel their leaders aren't holding up their end of the bargain. Negative behaviors such as job performance deviance and a lack of loyalty can emerge, directly resulting from this broken expectation.

In low-trust organizations, performance suffers because associates spend mental energy coping with the effects of toxic leadership rather than focusing on productive efforts.

Plus, in the absence of trust, associates are more likely to seek different employment opportunities, leading to poor retention rates.

Organizations that do not actively remove or mitigate toxic leadership (individuals or traits) should not expect sustained performance or pro-organization behaviors from their associates. Not just because the expectation is unrealistic, but also because studies have shown self-doubt, high levels of stress, anxiety, depression, and even physical symptoms, can be a direct result of toxic leadership and the breaking of the anticipated mutual trust.[35]

If you want to become an organization where people thrive—and stay—you have to eliminate toxic, abusive, or destructive leadership traits so that you can build and sustain trust with your associates. This brings us to the next two quadrants within the Culture Recovery Framework that focus entirely on creating a sustainable cycle of trust, both on an individual level and an organizational level.

As stated by Stephen M.R. Covey, in his book *Speed of Trust*, trust is built on two key components: capability trust and moral trust.[36] Within the Culture Recovery Framework, individual trust is about associates believing their leader has both their best interests at heart (moral trust) and the professional ability to help them achieve their goals (capability trust).

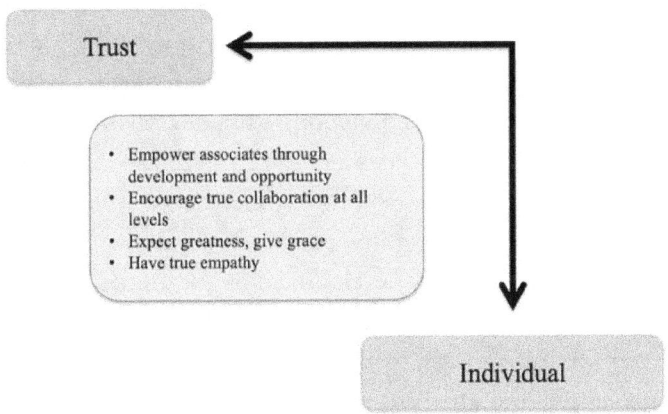

Keep in mind, you cannot skip ahead to this quadrant and start there. For this framework to be effective, you have to establish accountability before you can work on the individual trust principles. Why? Because accountability focuses on consistent, reliable behaviors, while trust delves into the intentions behind those behaviors. *Accountability fuels trust.* Once accountability has been established, you can move to this quadrant and focus on implementing the below individual trust principles.

1. Empower Associates through Development and Opportunity

Depending on the organization, this can be a difficult concept for many leaders to put into practice. Development is something that organizations use to attract talent, yet they do not necessarily have a specific plan to apply this promised development to all associates.

The simplest way to make this a priority is by identifying high-potential talent and offering them stretch assignments or cross-training opportunities. The challenge here is that most associates are hired to fulfill specific roles or needs. If they are good at what they do, or even simply meet the minimum requirements, they may not necessarily be in consideration for development opportunities because good people are needed within those roles. Leaders might even say this directly to the associate! Telling them they are simply "too good" to put anywhere else and that they are "needed" in this position. While this seems like a compliment, in my experience, this is actually perceived by the associate population as a lack of interest or care in their development, and it devalues the promises made for developmental opportunities in the organizations recruiting efforts.

Poor development opportunities can be most easily identified in associate reviews. I recommend analyzing your review process and considering these questions:

- When leaders meet with their direct reports, is there a genuine desire to help everyone improve?
- Is this reflected in real goals and opportunities for someone to grow?
- Does the associate participate in the conversation?
- Are associate needs and wants taken into consideration?
- Has the organization utilized internal or external consultation to identify best-in-class behaviors, skills, and attributes for each role?

- Has the organization provided a clear pathway for both leaders and associates to work towards any skill attainment they lack?

By actively developing all team members, not only does the overall competency and performance of the team improve, but it also changes the perception of leadership's commitment to the entire organization. I am not suggesting that every person be put on a path to elevate through the ranks. Not everyone has the innate ability or even desire to take that journey. Yet, organizational leadership should continually provide opportunities for that individual contributor to be better at their role day after day.

2. Encourage True Collaboration at Each Level of the Organization

Collaboration, though often untrained in many organizations, can be a powerful tool for building trust between individuals when actively taught and reinforced. When we look at our closest relationships, they often involve individuals with whom we have shared strife or contention, whether in conflict with each other or from facing a mutual adversity. Shared difficulties or tragedies build a level of intimacy that casual relationships cannot replicate. This is why military veterans who have served in combat exhibit a unique devotion to each other—even if they didn't know each other personally—simply because they had a shared difficult experience.

In professional environments, shared challenges and conflicts can similarly foster trust. When individuals experience and resolve conflicts together, it fosters a deeper sense of trust and camaraderie, strengthening relationships and enhancing teamwork. In fact, I even use this in my professional sales training and teach techniques that will purposely create temporary conflict or tension so that the sales executive can resolve it and build trust with their client.

In collaboration there will be tension and potential conflict. When these conflicts are resolved in a healthy manner, rather than ignored or swept under the rug, the conflict can build and support trust between associates and leaders. To this end, wise leaders may even find reason to challenge assumptions or to disagree (without being disagreeable) with associates to allow the associate to better articulate and defend their viewpoints so they may grow and resolve the conflict together. Liz Wiseman comments in her book that wise leaders seek to foster debate, view a scenario from every angle, and to challenge assumptions, because they know it will foster camaraderie.[37]

Limiting collaborative activities to senior leader conference rooms misses the opportunity to build trust across all levels of the organization. Instead, organizations should make it a priority to teach all associates how to appropriately collaborate and experience trust at an early stage of their organizational tenure. This way, they are far more likely to have refined this skill as their career progresses.

3. Expect Greatness, Give Grace

Too often, associates in our organizations feel that they are consistently judged and evaluated on a pass/fail scale.

Be it a corporation or volunteer organization, we ask for certain goals to be met, and when they are not, we seem to be comfortable in letting the associate feel as if they have failed. Internally we may justify this, knowingly or not, as an opportunity for them to take personal accountability and work harder to achieve their goals next time. However, I suggest that this type of thinking is outmoded, immature, and limiting.

I am not remotely suggesting that we soften goals or expectations, or that we shouldn't expect greatness and accountability from our teams. Rather, we should expect those things *and* we should anticipate that some, or perhaps even most of the time, the individual may come up short. When that happens, we need to have a discussion with the associate and develop a plan moving forward that mutually recognizes the results gap but doesn't imply failure.

We may instinctively think that failure will motivate someone to work harder, but the reality is that many will simply give up or refuse to try again due to how they felt upon failing. As a member of Generation X, I often reflect on our self-sufficient upbringing and realize that it is our generation that may have overcompensated with our children, by providing participation trophies and promoting the mindset that everyone's a winner. This has, unfortunately, led to many younger generations being labeled as entitled or weak by older generations. What many people within the older generations fail to realize is the possibility, opportunity, and value of creating an environment that encourages and celebrates winners and winning, while not making others feel diminished.

Giving grace means recognizing that the final desired goal and expectation has not changed, while also understanding that there is a process to accomplishment. It involves letting someone know that it is okay to ask for help with a difficult assignment, without the expectation that they know everything immediately. It means separating someone's performance on a task from their worth as a human. When an individual fails to meet an expectation, there should be nothing in our response that makes them feel small or less about themselves. In fact, we have a moral obligation to help them overcome any negative feelings they may have about their performance.

In my experience, this principle, applied consistently, creates a deep sense of individual trust oftentimes referred to as "loyalty," which is a trait many leaders crave but can't seem to achieve with their associates. This sense of loyalty remains out of their reach because they expect it without holding themselves accountable, building trust, or giving any grace to those they lead.

4. Have True Empathy

I once worked for a multi-billion-dollar firm in which my experience was one of collaboration and mutual trust with the team I worked on. I had mistakenly assumed this was the norm throughout the organization, but I was wrong. At a pivotal time for the organization, the leadership of this company made a decision that unintentionally devalued a large percentage of the associates by establishing a new minimum educational requirement for a particular level of roles. Logically, I understood the desire to upscale this particular role. However, it marginalized many associates who had been with the team the longest, effectively eliminating all future opportunities for their growth.

While I didn't agree with this decision, what bothered me most was the lack of inclusion of individuals who had differing perspectives and were closer to the field. Their feedback could have prevented the *hundreds* of associate resignations that shortly followed this decision, with most of this desirable talent going to our nearest competitors. I fully recognize that I became emotionally involved, especially since I had extended a promotion offer to someone, and then had to rescind the offer due to this policy change (even after the promotion had been publicly announced). But perhaps more effectual to me, this experience shattered my trust in certain members of organizational leadership and severely impacted my relationships with others who felt this decision was best made in a vacuum, without any efforts to develop buy-in or to understand those who it affected.

This was the exact opposite of empathy. Most savvy executives have a working demonstration of empathy; however, empathy may not be demonstrated in their daily behavior, or as an expectation of other senior leaders by way of accountability. This superficial version of empathy is shown by using field-level terminology to feign a perception that "I am one of you," which leaders often use. But rarely do field-level associates expect senior leadership to know what it's like to function in their day-to-day role. Instead, associates expect that the leadership will gain appropriate field perspectives before making a major decision so this knowledge can guide their strategy. Which means that showing empathy might look like senior leaders going into the field as an opportunity to see through the eyes of the rest of the team.

There is much talk about empathy in public forums, especially regarding inclusion and class divisions within organizations. We applaud leaders who—while in their expensive suits—bend down to pick up trash or book their own travel arrangements because we collectively long for the comfort that comes when we believe that organizational leadership understands our opportunities and challenges. But many leaders haven't truly looked at the challenges of those in the field and have an outdated understanding of the issues they face.

If our goal is to lead with empathy, we need to understand the associate experience from their perspective. This understanding is how we as leaders can help pull associates past their belief in themselves and beyond their current capabilities. If we fail to understand their experience, we will fail to guide others. Similar to a rock climber trusting their belay—the person at the bottom of the climb holding the rope, who both guides and supports the climber—we will struggle to pull people beyond their limitations, especially if they cannot trust that we will predictably and consistently support them with pure intentions for their benefit.

Once you have established these principles of individual trust, organizational trust naturally begins to take shape. Yet there are still guiding principles within this quadrant you can use to better establish organizational trust. Let's take a deeper look at the principles within this segment in the next chapter.

REFLECTIONS

Understand

1. In low-trust organizations, performance suffers, associates spend mental energy coping with the effects of toxic leadership rather than focusing on productive efforts
2. Individual trust is about associates believing their leader has both their best interests at heart and the professional ability to help them achieve their goals
3. Accountability fuels trust
4. Decisions made in a vacuum typically fail to achieve buy-in from the organization as a whole
5. If our goal is to lead with empathy, we need to understand the associate experience from their perspective

Act

1. Demonstrate how to disagree, without being disagreeable
2. Empower associates through development opportunity

3. Encourage true collaboration at all levels
4. Expect greatness, but give grace
5. Have true empathy

9

CULTURE RECOVERY FRAMEWORK— ORGANIZATIONAL TRUST

O rganizational trust is both a representation of consistency, and the maturity, of the other three quadrants. As we move from demonstrating organizational and individual accountability, we then grow to develop one-one-one trust. The next level—the greater level of trust, and this quadrant of the Culture Recovery Framework—is organizational trust, which comes when individuals believe that the organization, not just certain individuals, will act in their best interest.

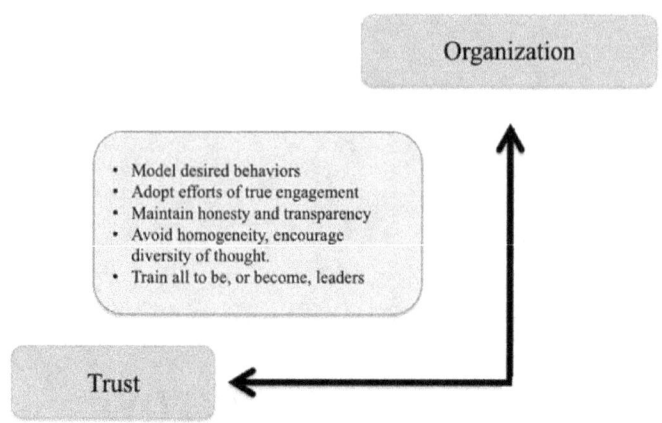

In my consulting work, I have regularly seen organizations who want to skip to this quadrant and demonstrate the behaviors that support organizational trust, yet they find themselves lacking in the desired results simply because they have not focused on the behaviors (established in the other three quadrants) that lead them to a place where their actions have the intended outcome. Organizational trust is hard to earn if you have not first worked your way through the other three quadrants. However, if you are following the Culture Recovery Framework, and have worked your way through the other subsequent quadrants, here are the principles you should follow to help establish organizational trust:

1. Model Desired Behaviors

As humans, we tend to find it easy(ish) to adjust our approach when dealing with different individuals. This person-to-person flexibility supports the various types of interactions and relationships we have with those around us. But as a leader, we need to maintain a certain level of consistency across all public and private activities through the many varied circumstances we face in our organization. This can be extremely challenging; however, when done well, this leads to an outcome where your modeled behaviors are so consistent that members of the organization may even use those attributes to describe you.

I once worked with an organization that had a split leadership model directly reporting to the owner. One of these leaders, focusing on operations, did not regularly exhibit the behaviors that he expected of others. His day would consist of coming in around 9:00 am, often after his team was already there. His first hour or so would be spent reading the newspaper, and then he would dig into various reports regarding business metrics. I recognize that my view and time with this leader was minimal, but I rarely saw him in any team engagements, other than when he thought there was something wrong. There was no engagement with customers and very limited urgency, though he would expect urgency out of others. I believe he cared for the associates and the company, though it was hardly discernible by his calendar.

In contrast, the other senior leader was highly engaged. The same reports were reviewed, the same difficult conversations were had, but there was a different sense that this leader acted as a partner to the team. Much of his time was spent outside the office, in the field meeting with customers, and assisting in sales and service conversations. Though an executive with the company, even his travel included two-star hotels with free breakfast, simply because he didn't want to appear to be more entitled than his team. Individuals who left that firm for any reason consistently continued to respect this second leader for his approach and modeled behaviors. This leader's example has been a model I have tried to emulate.

Both leaders were consistent, but only one was consistent in the desired behaviors that associates want to see from those who lead them. This made that leader a memorable model of an ethical leader that many remembered long after they stopped working with him.

2. Adopt Efforts of True Engagement

In other quadrants, we discussed activities around associate surveys, seeking open dialogue, and acting on findings. As we seek to develop organizational trust, these individual activities often evolve from specific actions to address toxicity to become a cultural norm, fully expected and predictable.

In this step, we need to move beyond these programmatic activities. One-to-one relationships are often developed in earlier quadrants; this quadrant represents the one-to-many relationship. For example, when leaders leave their offices and spend time in the field or on the production floor, they make connections with individuals that can generate self-perpetuating goodwill. In addition to gaining insight from the team, being present in their workspace helps to remove class barriers and internal segmentation.

Frankly, these opportunities to connect are rarely spontaneous. Rather they should be scheduled to ensure they get done. This might be something as simple as having a calendar alert or alarm to remind you a couple times of day to get up and go talk to people outside of your specific office or cubicle. You could also block out extended portions of your calendar to devote the time necessary to be in the field. This includes visiting difficult areas where your presence is required to challenge assumptions or demonstrate urgency. It also involves expressing gratitude to a stable team or department.

As a leader, especially one with a visible role and title, it can be easy to underestimate the influence you wield by your presence. I once had a colleague remind me in an afterhours mixer that my presence there wasn't about me, but rather was for me to have the opportunity to make connections with others and to show my appreciation to them. I appreciated this counsel, as I'm not overly extroverted as an individual and would likely have gone home from the mixer as quickly as possible. These words helped me realize the responsibility of my role and to take my eyes off myself so I could invest socially in the team.

3. Maintain Honesty and Transparency

Assuming the Culture Recovery Framework has helped leaders exhibit candor and transparency in organizational matters (including the realities of toxicity they seek to overcome), this is a continuation of the practice of transparency.

Earlier mentions of this behavior were meant to demonstrate leaders' self-awareness and reflection. A continued practice of honesty and transparency further shows a commitment to proactive communication and belief in those being addressed. The organizational members must come to trust that leadership will continue in their openness. A failure to continue this behavior initially results in a vacuum where any number of self-derived narratives may grow into rumors and groupthink. When the associates experience consistently open leaders who suddenly become closed-off and inclusive, this will lead to associates feeling excluded or even make them feel (or even fear) information is being withheld from them. This shift may be viewed more harshly by the associate population than if no transparency had existed at all and can lead to an increase in deviant behaviors.

However, I will add, while honesty and transparency must be the direction, there is wisdom in the appropriate application of filters and recognition of your audience. Transparency is required with delivery in mind.

I was recently in a meeting where a group of managers expressed some operational concerns they were facing. While these issues were outside of my span of control, I chose to let the conversation continue so that I could both better understand where this group was coming from, and to allow them to speak in such a way that they could feel heard. In hindsight, I wasn't aware of all that were participating in that meeting. I was addressing the management group that was immediately in front of me and was unaware there was also a camera and microphone in the room for the support staff which were attending remotely.

The degree in which the managers expressed their concerns, often with heavy emotions attached, was more than what was likely appropriate for the support staff. Of course, they are adults as well, but many were new to the organization. They did not have the same understanding of the role of a manager, and as such did not know how to prioritize or weigh the various concerns being shared by the managers, some of which were entirely self-inflicted challenges.

By applying a filter, we don't seek to hide the realities of the organization from the associates as they very likely see everything that we see. Rather, we consider the delivery in such a way that we can simultaneously show awareness alongside an exhibition of hope and excitement for the future. We shouldn't sweep things under the rug or pretend that the elephant isn't in the room, but we don't need to act as if all is lost, regardless of the challenges discussed. Admittedly, it can be a difficult balance.

4. Avoid Homogeneity, Encourage Diversity of Thought

Homogeneity is a state of sameness where individuals socially and culturally become so near to each other that uniqueness and diversity fade away. This often occurs in organizations when hiring managers tend to gravitate towards individuals who think and act the same. Unknowingly, they justify these hires based on "cultural fit," yet they fail to recognize those they hired were a comfort level fit.

Instinctively, we may not like to be challenged by others. When others come into our sphere who perceive the world around us differently, they may be likely to challenge our assumptions, and that is not typically comfortable. When we hire someone who is the same as us, we assume—inadvertently or not—they will be easier to manage because they will think and act like us.

The antithesis of homogeneity is diversity of thought. Politically and in the current public zeitgeist, social diversity is viewed most often as demographics; however, these factors may lead to varied perspectives but are not necessarily diversity of thought in and of themselves. Several individuals who may have varied demographic attributes, but perceive circumstances the same, can still lead to fixed mindsets, a term coined by Dr. Carol Dweck,[38] which we want to avoid through diversity of thought.

When sought after, economic, racial, and similar demographic diversity may be excellent ways to accomplish the goal of diverse opinions and perspectives within the organization. Regardless of the variety of categories that individuals may place themselves in, it is the leader's responsibility to extract from each individual their own understanding and opinions. If the culture is not supportive of people speaking up, challenging the ongoing narrative, or sharing an opposing viewpoint, then the organizational population will devolve to a single talking point.

Embracing diversity of thought means creating an environment where differing opinions are not only tolerated, but encouraged. It involves fostering a culture where associates feel safe to express their ideas and where their contributions are genuinely valued. This can lead to more innovative solutions, as a variety of perspectives will provide new insights and approaches to problem-solving.

5. Train All to Be or to Become Leaders

It is a moral responsibility for leadership to provide development opportunities for each associate. This is a fundamental aspect of building individual trust. Yet, many associates don't receive this training because they don't want to become leaders or don't qualify for the position. I would argue that regardless of their role or title, leadership is about the ability to influence, and has nothing to do with your rank in the organization. Therefore, leadership development opportunities should be available for every associate, regardless of their position in the organization.

While those being developed may certainly become qualified, or have an individual desire for elevated roles, this development is more about empowerment and personal ownership. When individuals feel as if they have a voice, and are being developed, they are more likely to act in the interests of the organization because their personal needs are met. This also works to build resiliency when organizational matters may not be going as well as everyone would like. This same resiliency supports a longer view and broader perspective of the circumstances around them.

Leadership training should encompass a variety of skills, including communication, conflict resolution, decision-making, and emotional intelligence, and it should not be specially reserved for those moving into management positions. By equipping all associates with these skills, you create a more adaptable and capable workforce filled with associates who are confident in their abilities and are more likely to step up in times of need, support their colleagues, or contribute positively to the organization's culture.

Additionally, fostering a culture where leadership is a shared responsibility rather than a hierarchical position encourages collaboration and collective problem-solving.

It breaks down silos and empowers everyone to contribute to the organization's success. Ultimately, training each individual to be, or to become, a leader reinforces the organizational trust and accountability we aim to build. It ensures that everyone, regardless of their position, understands their role in shaping and maintaining a healthy, productive culture.

FINAL THOUGHTS ON THE CULTURE RECOVERY FRAMEWORK

This entire book has been about avoiding, mitigating, or recovering from toxic leadership; or in other words, changing the focus from oneself to those around them and the organization as a whole.

Beyond simply teaching leadership principles or techniques, these efforts are about elevating the associate conversation. This involves specifically teaching the principles of the Culture Recovery Framework to *everyone* in the organization, which will act as a key tool in mitigating future toxic leadership concerns. By equipping the entire organization with the skills to think outwardly and gain a deeper understanding of what self-interested leaders look like, you create mutual accountability between leadership and associates. This cycle reinforces the organization's accountability to the individual and vice versa.

In chapter eleven, I will outline additional case studies of organizations that have successfully implemented the Culture Recovery Framework. These case studies will highlight the challenges they faced and the successes they found. As you bring this framework to your own organization, I encourage you to think about how accountability, trust, and ethical leadership can transform your organization *and* your personal approach to leadership.

Remember, the journey towards a healthier organizational culture starts with intentional actions and a commitment to continuous improvement. By embracing these principles and applying them consistently, you are not just preventing toxicity—you are building a resilient, high-trust environment where every associate feels valued and empowered to contribute their best.

REFLECTIONS

Understand

1. Organizational trust is when individuals believe that the organization, not just certain individuals, will act in their best interest
2. Opportunities to connect are rarely spontaneous and should instead be scheduled in your calendar
3. The absence of consistent candor in communication allows groupthink and false narratives to thrive
4. Know your audience; transparency must take into account the delivery

Act

1. Model desired behaviors
2. Adopt efforts of true engagement
3. Maintain honesty and transparency
4. Avoid homogeneity and encourage diversity of thought
5. Train everyone to be a leader

PART
3

SUSTAINABLE HEALING

ontinuing with my initial story about the two organizations, one acquiring the other: As we identified
and understood the conditions that allowed for toxic
behaviors to flourish, we progressed through the four-
stages of the Culture Recovery Framework.

With specific purpose, we sought for a level of organizational accountability. While pride, perfectionism, and status
dominated the past public and private persona of corporate
leadership, we instead presented openness and candor. We
spoke boldly of where we had been, transparently sharing
our failings alongside the victories. We altered our top-
down hierarchy in favor of a flatter organization, and one
where each role understood that their leadership had an
expectation to serve their direct reports. Rather than rest-
ing only upon high associate engagement and satisfaction
scores, we added recurring focus groups of individuals from
a cross-section of the organization that could help us better
know what the team was thinking and feeling.

Part of this effort in creating feedback loops was to
know how we would react if we received criticism for any

past or current actions taken by a member of the team or the organization. Even if we didn't agree, or perhaps we had some other business constraint that prohibited making a change, how would we ensure that the associate felt safe in sharing their concern, and validated in what was shared?

When we found something that we could adjust, we did so with urgency. If something wasn't possible to change, for any given reason, we followed up with the concerned individual or team. We shared with them both the what and the why. A failure to act, or a failure to follow up, would reduce our opportunities to gain trust and buy-in for our other efforts, so we made this a priority.

An aspect of this effort was to break down the various classes that existed between different staff roles. Some of the organizations could be considered blue collar and field centric. In the old model, these groups often did not cross over, and there were various levels of status, or even resentment, between them. To break down these barriers, we needed a multi-faceted approach.

We first employed efforts to ensure that there was a cross-experiential pattern. Office people spent time in the field, field staff spent time in the office. We highlighted the value that each role contributed, while reinforcing that no position was superior to another. However, this wasn't enough. Many organizations talk about training and development for growth, but we needed to ensure that everyone knew their path. Using a consultant to help identify the best-in-class skill sets and attributes of each role in the organization, we produced a roadmap so that anyone, anywhere in the organization, knew exactly what skills and behaviors would be necessary for success in any role.

This then became part of our annual goal setting and evaluation process. Rather than check-the-box transactional conversations around performance once or twice per year, each manager was expected to know the desired trajectory of everyone on their team, and they were accountable to report out on what they were doing as a leader to help their team grow. A portion of each month was spent in helping that individual grow. Even if someone was in their desired role, they would still be expected to be better each successive month.

A crucial aspect of these efforts was continually cultivating diversity of thought. While we strived to continue the previously mentioned behaviors with the existing team, we also willfully and purposely sought out individuals to add to the organization who had different, but complementary skill sets and ideas.

Rather than taking the easy route of hiring people we knew, or those that thought as we did, job candidates were sourced whose experience and circumstances would force us to challenge our developed notions. Admittedly, this was often uncomfortable at first, but we truly wanted to interact with individuals who had a different perspective on what we were doing as a business and how we might best accomplish our goals. As we did this, we found that our understanding of certain skills and leadership types shifted. Rather, it became less about hiring for a particular fit or type, and instead shifted to more honestly seeking what might otherwise be missing.

To many readers, all this people-centeredness may seem to be too philosophical, progressive, or absent of the results orientation that most businesses strive for. But in truth, the results are contrary to popular belief. A healthy and robust ethical culture can more effectively produce those results and will do so in exponential and sustainable ways.

In the organization discussed over these three preceding sections, we managed to double the annual revenue within *three years*. This is with a firm that had been in business for nearly seventy years. In addition to doubling revenue, we increased the EBITDA margin by 3x. Simultaneously, the larger parent organization had a tumultuous existence including two CEO changes, an entire swap of the C-Suite, and numerous internal scandals and lawsuits.

Upon my departure for another assignment, a new leader was brought in from inside of a crony-relationship from the parent organization. This self-oriented leader worked hard to exert their self-interested agenda, and this caused some of the ethical subordinate leaders to leave the organization. However, most stayed. That said, thankfully a pattern of culture had already been firmly rooted in the organization centered around trust and accountability, and it now existed outside any single leader. When the organizational culture was incongruent with hostile motives, this toxic and self-interested leader left the organization.

From my understanding, this firm is resoundingly healthy several years later, and a shining example within the network of the parent corporation. This wasn't about me, but rather a consistent and persistent effort by the whole team and the use of a framework that was pro-organization—ultimately a system by which individuals felt genuinely valued and professionally-developed based on both their desires and effort.

The antithesis of the toxic leader is the ethical leader. It takes ethical leaders to build an ethical culture, and ethical cultures do much to mitigate the risks of toxic leaders. It is possible, and highly likely, to achieve stakeholder value by lifting an organization through its people. This is the key for sustainable growth for years to come, and it is the reason why the Culture Recovery Framework has successfully solved for associate retention and culture recovery in many organizations.

10

INTENTION IS REQUIRED

Recovering from toxicity will undoubtedly be challenging because we aren't dealing with processes or systems alone; we're dealing with *humans*.

Each individual in an organization will be affected differently by a toxic environment, and each will require a tailored approach to support their recovery. Culture recovery is not a one-size-fits-all solution at the individual level, and it cannot happen passively. Intention, empathy, and consistency should be used alongside the Culture Recovery Framework to restore a healthy organizational culture and to prevent future toxicity

BEHAVIOR CHANGE IS DIFFICULT

Throughout this book, I've tried to convey that many of these concepts and principles may sound obvious. These may be things that leaders assume they, or their teams, are already doing. But the reality is that many of the behaviors outlined don't often translate into what happens in the real life demands of daily operations. Just like when someone is desperately trying to get to a meeting on time but are late because they are blocked by someone who is *fully* committed to obeying the speed limit, any number of issues can distract us from the crucial matters of people and culture. It's easy to get sidetracked by these immediate and pressing concerns when you have mile long to-do lists and calls to make.

I hope every reader has connected with several of the concepts discussed so far. However, more important than receiving an "ah-ha!" moment that propels you to change is the execution within your organization. It's not enough to act on the principles that stood out or were meaningful to you; following the *entire plan* is necessary to cultivate the desired outcomes. Partial efforts only lead to partial results. Yet, this is exactly what happens when well-meaning leaders seek to implement behavior change without first changing thoughts, understanding, and perceptions. Without this holistic approach, their efforts will likely be ineffective and may even be perceived as patronizing.

With all of this said, these techniques cannot be diminished to tasks to be completed. Rather, these are behavioral changes that start with adjusting how we as leaders think and perceive, which ultimately affects our behaviors and how our messages are received. If we fail to recognize that these improvements require a change of thought, then we will fail to recognize the outcomes we seek. We cannot surge forward with high velocity and momentum without direction. Put another way: if we want to change results or outcomes, we can best accomplish this by influencing behaviors; if we want to change how people feel, we need to help others (and ourselves) change the way we think.

Behavior change is inherently difficult because it involves altering deeply ingrained habits, mindsets, and automatic responses that have been shaped over years of experience. This process requires a conscious and sustained effort, often in the face of resistance from both individuals and the organizational culture. Even when the minutiae of the day-to-day concerns press in on you. Start by looking inward. What are you doing today that you need to stop doing tomorrow? Keep that behavior in mind, even when your plate is piled high with to-dos. Make it non-negotiable. If you do this, slowly, but surely, you will see these behavior changes take root.

OLD WOUNDS WILL LIMIT NEW EFFORTS

For any of us who have experienced financial difficulties, which—let's be honest, we all have at one point or another—you know it's difficult to consider how to invest your money when you don't have enough to pay your bills. Trust operates similarly. A lack of trust doesn't just create a negative balance; it actively impedes progress, making everything more challenging, costly, and less effective. When trying to rebuild a damaged culture, you will be starting from a place of deficit and working your way up to a neutral ground.

Psychologically, this can be daunting for new leaders who enter their roles with the best intentions and a wealth of energy, only to feel hampered by the lingering consequences of previous toxic leadership. When the entire culture is toxic, the new leader might feel like they're trying to plant trees in the desert. Until the environment becomes more hospitable, their efforts will feel futile and the fruits of their labor nonexistent.

However, this does not mean the effort isn't worthwhile. On the contrary, once the threshold of trust is overcome, the leader may find themselves more effective than if trust had always been present. This might initially seem counterintuitive, especially when early outcomes are limited by past damage. Yet, individuals within the organization will observe your determination to overcome the inherited negativity, and when they watch you overcome the hand you've been dealt, they will trust you more.

As you fight to overcome past negativity and poor behaviors, just know that you will have an accelerating curve of results. Those results will be miniscule or perhaps unnoticeable for far longer than you would like. However, if you are consistent in your effort and message, the results will come. And when they do come, they will be far greater than you could ever expect.

YOUR ASSOCIATES WILL HAVE DOUBTS

If you have stepped into the role of a department lead within a department that has undergone multiple leadership changes in a short span, you will face unfair doubts. I say unfair, not because the associates shouldn't have those doubts—the leaders before them have likely failed them continually, so their doubts are valid—but unfair because they will be placed on your shoulders before you have a chance to prove yourself.

When this happens, remember, each new leader arrived in this department or company with grand expectations of change and improvement, only to leave without making any lasting impact. Or worse, only to leave after they inflict toxic and controlling behaviors on their associates. As a result, the associates in this department have understandably become jaded, and will likely view any new initiatives with suspicion and doubt.

When you step into this new leadership role and announce a series of changes aimed at fostering a more inclusive and supportive work environment, including regular feedback sessions, transparent communication about company goals, and opportunities for professional development, you will notice a lack of enthusiasm and engagement from your team. They might even say, "We've heard this all before." In these situations, our gut response is often frustration, or even annoyance. This doubt can be deeply deflating to new leaders—which is why I want to warn you that it will happen, so you can prepare yourself. As the leader seeking an effective change, you must be cognizant and empathetic to the past experiences of those on your team. Even when the doubt isn't deserved, even when it can be frustrating or annoying.

If you fail to exhibit empathy, your actions will be judged as patronizing or pandering. Each follower in the organization will need to go through their own journey towards the unified organizational direction, and their initial doubt is part of that journey. An effective ethical leader should find an opportunity to purposefully exhibit empathy to those who doubt their intentions and to help acknowledge the frustrations of their associates. You need to validate these feelings to help associates move through the healing process and grow their trust in your leadership.

EVERY LEADER LEAVES A MARK

In some of my consulting efforts, I have watched new leaders enter an organization with every intention and every necessary skill to help the team recover, especially in acquisitions or company mergers, where time spent solidifying the new culture is crucial. They have it all, and they make significant changes for the company. Yet, those same companies start to backslide into previous toxic behaviors once this leader moves on. This is because even though the leader was effective, the expected behaviors of an ethical culture were not solidified well enough to outlast the ethical leader's tenure. Then perhaps the next leader who took over focused on their own agenda, disregarding the efforts of the previous ethical leader, further devolving the organization.

For culture change to take root, the new culture-changing leader must remain within the organization long enough for the behaviors to become part of the accepted cultural norm, *and* the next leader must be equally willing and able, and expected, to carry the same torch.

This isn't to suggest that the second leader shouldn't have their own vision for the organization. They absolutely should walk their own unique path. But whatever direction they take the company, they should continue to promote and demonstrate the desired ethical behaviors the previous leader emulated.

Each new leader leaves a mark. They will either add to or negate the ethical culture and leadership efforts. This is why the Culture Recovery Framework needs to seep into every level of the organization. It isn't enough to stop at leadership. The culture needs to be strong enough to point out toxicity as soon as it happens or repel toxicity altogether. That way, those leaders that might tear apart the hard work of creating an accountable, high trust culture never land in positions of leadership.

ADDRESSING TOXICITY WILL INCREASE PROFIT

Unfortunately, in today's world, many associates feel as if they are simply tools wielded at the leadership's whim. They feel disregarded, disrespected, stuck, and undervalued. This will always lead to deviant behaviors and poor performance because that is often one of the only ways for associates to cope with such toxic environments without getting fired. We've likely all had a boss that we hated, at a job we despised—but needed—so we came in and only performed the bare minimum of our job duties. We didn't look for ways to innovate, we didn't feel like we had any opportunity to grow, and we certainly didn't perform to the best of our ability. This is a natural consequence of toxicity, and it will affect your profit margin.

Following the Culture Recovery Framework will add to your organization's profit because it transforms human capital from a tool into a valued resource.

Everything we have discussed is about recovering or improving the culture in your organization to such a degree that the people who make the organization function want to participate in its goals. Employment alone is no indication of performance or intent to act in the best interests of the organization. For true engagement and high performance to be realized, the organization must first provide a culture that is worthy of the associates' time and energy. When associates stop feeling as if they are merely tools and realize they are highly valued individuals, performance will increase.

As leaders, we should mature beyond the notion that human capital is merely a commoditized resource. Conversations suggesting that losing one person is insignificant because they can easily be replaced must be left behind. Instead, if we aim to attract and retain the very best talent, regardless of the level of skill required for a particular role, we need to actively consider the environment we provide.

This environment is not created in boardrooms or planning sessions, but rather in the day-to-day interactions between leaders and associates.

No gardener would expect a healthy crop to grow in unhealthy soil. Similarly, leaders cannot expect associates to meet their expectations when they take little care in nurturing the work environment. By addressing toxicity and fostering a positive culture, leaders lay the groundwork for a more engaged, productive, and ultimately profitable organization.

As we move into the final chapter of this book, I want to provide you with key examples of the Culture Recovery Framework in action. The previous chapters have taught you the strategies, given you examples, and paved the way for your understanding. But I am a true believer of offering real life examples of the Culture Recovery Framework in action so you can better see how it could affect your organization. Let's take a further look at companies who have put the Culture Recovery Framework to the test.

REFLECTIONS

Understand

1. Assess your leadership team, they should have complementary skill sets that will assist in broader human connections *and* business acumen

2. A healthy and robust ethical culture will effectively produce good business results in exponential and sustainable ways

3. It takes ethical leaders to build an ethical culture, and ethical cultures do much to mitigate the risks of toxic leaders

4. If we want to change how people feel, we need to help others, and ourselves, change the way we think

5. Human capital is more than a commoditized resource

Act

1. Purposely seek out new individuals for your team that represent new ideas

2. Identify best-in-class attributes and skills for each role in your organization, and share these with everyone

3. Demonstrate the intention, empathy, and consistency that should be used alongside the Culture Recovery Framework to restore a healthy organizational culture and to prevent future toxicity

4. Fight beyond the negativity of the past to experience the exponential results that come

5. Stay consistent to the Culture Recovery Framework principles to ensure that the behaviors and mindsets solidify into the upgraded culture

11

CASE MANAGEMENT FUNCTION

I n this chapter, I have curated four case studies analyzing each quadrant of the Culture Recovery Framework in the order that I recommend moving through the framework. The first case study revolves around organizational accountability, the second around individual accountability, the third around individual trust, and the fourth around organizational trust.

My hope is that within these different case studies, you'll see the Culture Recovery Framework at work and maybe even see some of the issues your organization faces within them. Keep in mind, names of organizations and people have been removed for privacy reasons, but each of these stories come from my consulting efforts when implementing the Culture Recovery Framework.

CASE STUDY #1–ASSUMING THE MANTLE OF ACCOUNTABILITY

I consulted for a firm in the Pacific Northwest that struggled significantly with associate retention. We started by exploring the company's people-performance metrics together with their executive team. In the preceding year, they had experienced a greater than 100% turnover in their client-account managers! The financial expense associated with stay-bonuses, recruiting, premium pricing for new hires was egregious, in addition to the consequences of a 5x increase in their client loss rate.

We identified the primary cause that led to these accumulated challenges, but though the issue had been previously resolved, the consequences still lingered, and the prevailing emotion was one of defeat. The atmosphere was overtly negative, and our conversations focused on the overall attitude and morale of the organization.

I vividly remember one conversation where we discussed the relationship between leadership and the field associates, inclusive of their most recent internal satisfaction survey. One question was centered around whether the associates felt valued as a member of the organization. The score was surprisingly poor, especially given all the various initiatives and efforts that the leaders made. Not surprisingly, the leadership team was frustrated and perhaps even a little deflated from this result.

As we explored their various tactics to address this perception—both what had been done and what could be done—one leader in a comment of exasperation said,

"What more could we have done? What do they expect?" I replied, asking, "What did they say when you asked them?" I could near instantly sense a shift towards optimism in the room. They asked, "Can we do that?"

I digress for a moment: any associate or client surveys should be genuine and authentic. We should not "game the system" as warned by Fred Reichheld, Bain Fellow and creator of the Net Promoter System (NPS).[39] Our questions should be simple, direct, and not incentivized. When we artificially influence the inputs, we can no longer trust the outputs. Returning to our story, in their well-intended efforts seeking to not influence answers, the leadership team had misunderstood and neglected to follow up on findings to gain deeper insight.

This leadership team did two things immediately. First, they assembled a focus group of cross-functional staff and brought them in together to review this area of concern. The leadership spoke directly to the group, telling them that they appreciated the staff and had made efforts over the last year to demonstrate to the team that they were valued. However, the scores reflected that this value sentiment wasn't received as intended, and that leadership genuinely was concerned that the team felt this way. They then had an open and candid conversation with the group, free of justifications, judgments, or excuses. The leadership team found feedback that they could immediately apply, and they reviewed this information regularly in their meetings to ensure that they didn't fall into a trap by assuming that all was well. They continued to keep these ideas top of mind to ensure appropriate application.

The second thing this leadership team did was to come clean with everything that had happened in that last year. Previously and with the best of intentions, they never candidly spoke of the problems and hardships they faced. Things were viewed as being so bad that they didn't want to bring people down any further. However, too many on the team assumed that leadership simply didn't care or didn't know, and therefore in the absence of a conversation, they created their own story. When leadership began to speak of what happened, things changed. They didn't place blame or diminish those no longer with the company. They simply stated that this decision had been made, communication and execution was handled poorly, certain individuals chose to take advantage of it, and a cascade of consequences ensued.

Through their implementation of these two efforts, this firm regained the organizational accountability that was previously absent. They continued to work their way through the Culture Recovery Framework and have now found a consistency in people-performance and operational excellence. They would likely suggest they still have some distance to go, but it is that awareness they now possess that leads them forward in their culture shaping and associated business success.

CASE STUDY #2—SILENCE IS DISSENT

I had a client on the East Coast where an organization was owned as a portfolio company of a private equity firm.

The private equity firm asked that I spend some time evaluating the leadership of this portfolio company as they had only recently purchased controlling equity, and they wanted to know if the existing leadership team was appropriate for the growth they expected to occur within the company. This was a common assignment, so I thought I knew what to expect.

Upon arrival, I received a warm welcome by the executive team. They understood my role, and I didn't feel that they were posing or otherwise giving off a false image in hopes of saving their jobs. Rather, they seemed to be very candid in describing both their wins and their challenges. I was there as a strategic leadership and organizational consultant, not as a "hatchet man" looking for labor expenses to cut. Business metrics lined up with their descriptions, so all appeared to be as indicated. This itself was unique and well received, as oftentimes I find things have been swept under the rug pre-acquisition to make the operation appear more attractive.

However, my commission was to understand the viability of the team for the go-forward basis, under both the significant pressure to achieve business objectives, but also the extreme scrutiny that can accompany private-equity-backed firms where the firm partners are *on* the business, but not necessarily *in* the business. With no material concerns surfacing from my time spent with the leadership team, I began interviewing individuals in the second and third layers.

This was a several-decade old business in the consumer essential-services space. This business had blue collar field associates, middle management, back-office field and client support, and an accounting and finance division. My interviews, regardless of which department, were oddly similar. They didn't feel staged, though the responses I received were almost identical. More concerning was what they didn't say. No one shared any opportunities where the organization had failed or lacked self-reflection and growth.

As I continued to dig, I was finally able to crack a little bit of the armor of these good people, and the truth finally came through. While there was never anything I found to be ethically challenging, senior leadership believed that anyone expressing a concern was either whiny and lazy, or worse, disloyal. Having difficult conversations was not allowed, let alone encouraged or sought after. Collaboration didn't exist in their meetings, and senior leadership would talk *to* people, not *with* people.

Again, this wasn't a poor performing business. However, I could now easily report back as to why they had already reached their peak. They would not grow with this leadership team unless the leadership team was willing to dramatically adjust their thinking. It took some time to finally move past this reality. Without much turnover, there was a muscle memory of sorts where individuals in the firm didn't feel it was their place to point out the hazards that the new leadership could not see early in their role. Because of the culture solidified by the previous ownership, silence became the only means of dissent within the organization.

Beyond simply the application of the principals of the Culture Recovery Framework, this case is also an example of the resiliency required for such change. As mentioned, there was a lot of muscle-memory and ingrained habits. We provided training on exactly how to have difficult conversations, not simply tell them that the door was always open and that they were welcome to tell the leaders what was wrong. This led to predictable, consistent, and resilient accountability. The framework, applied with this far-sightedness, fueled the businesses evolution.

CASE STUDY #3—FRIENDLY FIRE AND A BREACH OF TRUST

Early in my career, I witnessed for myself the consequences of a self-interested leader. Unfortunately, that leader was me. At that stage of my progression, I was in the leadership pattern of command-and-control, relying upon guilt and veiled threats to "motivate" or generate urgency. I entered a role with a new firm to find a sales team that was already out of their element. Few, if any, were meeting their quotas. My field experiences with them suggested that they did not have any of the skills one would expect to find in a consistently successful salesperson. I had not yet learned to distinguish between a lack of skill vs. a lack of will, and I still thought people simply absorbed training and then went out and performed exactly what they learned.

I completely failed in my role of mentorship and coaching. There was accountability, but it was undeserved accountability as they were never equipped to succeed to begin with. I was also a diminisher by every measure.

At the end of my second month, at a sales meeting immediately following month-end, I gave the team a dose of "urgency" that I thought they needed. One individual, someone who was probably going through a difficult personal situation that I was unaware of, immediately blew up in a rage, demanding of me, "Are you actually going to help us, or are you just going to boss us around?!" That individual walked off the job after that meeting. Most others that were in the room that day left within a month or two.

I failed the company at that time, but more so, I failed those individuals. They may never have succeeded had they stayed, but they didn't get from me what they deserved. I was in their shoes once, yet I fully lacked empathy. I demonstrated to them the same horrible leadership that I received earlier in my career.

With the counsel of a wise mentor, I changed my approach (and thinking) around my role as a leader. It still took some years for me to formulate a pattern of behavior I could articulate, but I had at least begun the journey of making investments in other people. I began to arrive upon the realization that my charge as a leader was one of service, rather than merely administration. I still remember how I felt that day, almost thirty years ago now. I do wish I could find that individual and the team and apologize, but in lieu of that, I have committed to not repeating the same mistake.

In retrospect, I failed to fulfill the individual trust quadrant of the Culture Recovery Framework. They did not have any belief or expectations that my words and actions were for their benefit. And quite frankly, I don't know that they were at the time. I hadn't yet learned the power of trust in extracting the best performance from others, while also ensuring that my intentions were pure and for their benefit.

They knew I could sell, and when we were in the field together, I (unintentionally) flaunted how skilled I was in that space. I mistakenly thought that my demonstrations would give me credibility, thereby providing the justification that they should trust me. However, I never sought to build a relationship. I somehow thought they would grow and develop through osmosis and observation rather than authentic guidance, coaching, and appropriate accountability. Demonstration is important, but showing off is never a method for building individual trust or empowering others.

CASE STUDY #4–CONSISTENT AND PERSISTENT

An especially gratifying case of organizational trust occurred in the Central US. I was engaged by a parent company to support this regional organization out of what had been over a decade of declining and sub-par performance. Every example of what-not-to-do had been tried at this operation. They had a new company president every couple of years, and each came with an inflated ego that they were going to be the one to "fix it." Each new leader focused on operational excellence and looked for service model efficiencies. They added, changed, and implemented more technology, then they spent extreme sums of money in marketing attempts. None of this worked. Anyone who worked there didn't want to stay, and the customers knew it.

Back then, associate retention wasn't the buzzword it is today. In fact, it wasn't even considered in the firm. Everyone was replaceable, a commodity, and rarely viewed as worthy to breathe the air inside the office. On my first day at the office interviewing leaders, I was told of how an extremely high performing field worker had asked for a small raise because his wife recently became pregnant. The former president's reported response was, "A monkey could do your job, and you are lucky I even let you stay here!"

My role was external and third party, but the new president was eager to approach things differently. Success in this operation was a white whale of sorts, a puzzle that many had tried, and failed, to complete. This president was determined to win, and so I challenged him with a simple question: *If you could wipe the slate clean and start from scratch, what would the business look like, and how would you get there? Forget the rules, or what corporate restrictions might exist. In this vision, how do the associates think, act, and feel?*

With this leader's vision cast, and with their buy-in, the Culture Recovery Framework was set in motion. Things didn't change overnight. Years of distrust obstructed progress at times. However, persistence and consistency won people over. There were candid conversations and true engagement, and the pre-existence of the us vs. them mentality melted away. When individuals missed goals or made mistakes, people no longer feared retaliation. Accountability, and if appropriate, progressive discipline still existed, but it was balanced with a demonstrated care for the individual.

There was also a complete reorganization of their back-office team from a group of generalists to role-specific specialists. The teams in the field felt support from the office, and they also began to see the middle and senior management at their side in the field. Individuals from all parts of the organization were brought in to help review leadership's plans for new revenue lines or structure changes. Their insight and perspectives were included in planning, and they were openly regarded and given credit for their participation in the process.

Two years later, this operation which had previously been on every under-performer's list the parent company had, was now a shining example in the network. From sales, to delivery, to service, housed in this operation were some of the best individual contributors and teams in the industry. With a depth of leadership in the operation, growth opportunities became abundant for many others, resulting in promotions from all departments. Further, the primary leader I worked with consistently applied the principles of the Culture Recovery Framework in their own way, seeking to uplift all others around them. They found great success in this organization and advanced through many levels before choosing a path of entrepreneurship.

I am grateful I had the opportunity to watch this individual grow, and I am honored to see the value they bring to their firm, family, and community. But what's more powerful is that it all started with a leader who refused to accept the prior toxicity as the norm, found a way to change that norm, and implemented the Culture Recovery Framework so thoroughly that they curated a deep ethical culture within the organization. Through their actions, this leader changed hundreds of lives and elevated the organization.

CONCLUSION

The challenge of associate retention has become more pressing than ever. Despite the widespread recognition of this issue, many executive leaders and human capital practitioners struggle to address and rectify toxic leadership. They often fail to heal from its impacts and adjust their cultures to prevent such leadership from taking root again. This is where the Culture Recovery Framework comes into play.

We've discussed how superficial engagement efforts, such as annual associate satisfaction surveys and bonus plans tied to these scores, often miss the mark. These initiatives, while well-intentioned, tend to focus on improving metrics rather than genuinely transforming the associate experience. True change requires a deeper, more intentional approach—one that goes beyond surface-level fixes and addresses the root causes of toxicity.

The journey towards a healthier organizational culture begins with accountability. Leaders must exhibit humility, ownership, and self-awareness, acknowledging the deviations caused by toxic leadership and taking responsibility for rectifying them. This foundation of accountability paves the way for building trust, both at the individual and organizational levels. But addressing toxicity is not a one-time fix; it demands ongoing dedication. Old wounds and past experiences will influence how associates perceive and respond to new initiatives. Leaders must be empathetic and understand that healing takes time and persistence. The Culture Recovery Framework is designed to navigate these complexities, offering a structured approach to fostering accountability, trust, and an ethical organizational culture.

We have all likely experienced toxic leadership to some degree. This may have come from our professional pursuits, volunteer work, or even from our athletic coaches in our youth. No organization, whether professional or ecclesiastical, is immune from the risks associated with toxic leadership or toxic cultures. These issues arise not from the intentions of the organization but from individuals within that organization who prioritize their own agendas over the group's well-being. Rather than simply commiserating about our negative experiences, we should dig deep to understand how to fix these issues and prevent them from recurring.

The negativity in the world, especially after the COVID-19 pandemic, has led many to adopt a self-preservation mindset, often at the expense of others. It's an unfortunate twist on the golden rule—doing unto others *before* they do unto you. If I can help just one organization set a new standard of growth by prioritizing the development and well-being of its people, I hope it creates a ripple effect that leads to widespread positive change. When individuals experience what it is like to be part of an aligned team led by ethical leaders, they will forever change their expectations of how they should be treated and how they should treat others.

Throughout this book, we have explored the critical role of ethical leadership in shaping a healthy organizational culture. By following the principles outlined in the Culture Recovery Framework, you can create an environment where associates feel valued, supported, and motivated to contribute their best efforts. Ultimately, addressing toxicity will increase profitability by removing the transactional nature of human capital management and fostering an environment where associates are genuinely invested in the organization's success, leading to innovation, self-directed urgency, and sustainable growth.

This framework is tried and tested, backed by both academic research and practical application. It offers a roadmap for transforming your organization, healing from past toxicity, and preventing its recurrence. The journey may be challenging, but the rewards—both ethical and operational—are well worth the effort.

While I would love to sell millions of books—and of course, I'd recommend you buy several to share with your friends—this book is a personal and moral mission to upscale leadership capacity in general. Equipping organizations with the ability to recover or avoid toxic tendencies in their leaders and culture is my ultimate goal. The biggest reward I could receive is knowing that individuals are better off in their organizations than they would have been otherwise.

By committing to these principles and consistently applying them, you will see significant, sustainable results. The Culture Recovery Framework is your solution to the associate retention problem and the key to cultivating an ethical culture which talented associates seek to join. I believe with this framework you have the tools you need to build a brighter future for your organization. All you have to do is dedicate yourself to the change and follow the steps outlined in this book so you can become an ethical leader who brings out the best in those they serve.

ACKNOWLEDGMENTS

I n acknowledging those that have added value to this process, I admittedly am anxious to not forget anyone. This work alone has been monumental. However, it is a lifelong journey of learning and application that has brought me to this point in which I can share these strategies and stories with you.

Without exception, I honor my personal faith and give credit where it is due. Without Him, I am nothing. Similarly, I could never provide enough love, praise, and gratitude to my wife, Brooke, who is a brilliant executive coach, organizational psychologist, and wise counselor to me as I have put this all together. She, along with our children, Ethan, Layla, Ella, and Chase, have provided unending support through schooling, business ventures, excessive travel, and hours in front of a computer typing. To that end, I am immensely grateful to Danielle Harward at Alliance Ghostwriting for her hours of interviews and helping me to craft my message appropriately for print.

I have been a student of leadership for many years, taught to me in practice before I was even twenty years old. Business associates and mentors over the years taught me to devour the books from John Maxwell, David Sandler, Jim Collins, Stephen Covey, Dale Carnegie, Norman Vincent Peale, Og Mandino, and so many others. Later authors and speakers such as Simon Sinek, Timothy Clark, Brene´ Brown, Stephen M.R. Covey, and Liz Wiseman, helped me to frame my thoughts and learnings into more contemporary applications.

Many individuals from professional, personal, and ecclesiastical environments have added direct and personal counsel and mentorship to me. In no particular order, and my sincere apologies to those I neglect to include, I further express my gratitude to Jim Payne, Kirk Call, Matt Lattimer, Lance Martin, Chris Algiene, Julia Cronin-Gilmore, Steve Good, Kirk Marcy, Matthew Carpenter, and so many others.

Cheers to each of you!

REFERENCES

INTRODUCTION

1   Collins, J. (2021). *Good to Great*. Harper Business.
2   Hughes, B. C. (2022). Examining Toxic Leadership: An Integrated Framework for Organizational Recovery. *Journal of Behavioral and Applied Management, 33*(3).

CHAPTER 1: SHIFT IN MINDSET

3   Lee, T. W. (2018). Managing Employee Retention and Turnover with 21st Century Ideas. *Organizational Dynamics, 47*, 88-98.
4   Covey, S. M. (2008). *Speed of Trust*. Free Press.
5   Kaiser, R. B. (2008). Leadership and the fate of organizations. *American Psychologist, 63*, 96-110.
6   (2024, September 6). From Bureau of Labor Statistics: https://www.bls.gov/news.release/pdf/empsit.pdf
7   Mayer, K. (2023, May 13). From Society for Human Resource Management: https://www.shrm.org/topics-tools/news/benefits-compensation/job-satisfaction-high-thanks-to-work-life-balance-strides
8   Hughes, B. C. (2022). Examining Toxic Leadership: An Integrated Framework for Organizational Recovery. *Journal for Behavioral and Applied Management*, 309-344.
9   Tatel, C., & Wigert, B. (2024, July 10). From Gallup: https://www.gallup.com/workplace/646538/employee-turnover-preventable-often-ignored.aspx?utm_source=linkedin&utm_medium=o_social&utm_term=gallup&utm_campaign=li-wk-greatdetachment_p1_080124

10 Executive, H. R. (n.d.). *Engaging the Workforce Across Generations*. From Workday: https://forms.workday.com/en-us/whitepapers/engaging-the-workforce-across-generations/form.html?camp=7011B000002hK9e&eid=enus_ppc_wd_gg_hcm_hr_wp_17.1948&utm_medium=ppc&utm_source=gg&utm_campaign=paid+search+-+Engaging+the+Workforce+Across+Generations&pro

11 ibid.

CHAPTER 2: TOXIC LEADERSHIP

12 *1982 Thunderbirds Indian Springs diamond crash*. (2024, September 13). From Wikipedia: https://en.wikipedia.org/wiki/1982_Thunderbirds_Indian_Springs_Diamond_Crash

13 Grant, A. (2022, January 4). From X: https://x.com/AdamMGrant/status/1478399527723970564

14 Matos, K., O'Neill, O., & Lei, X. (2018). Toxic leadership and the masculinity contest culture: How "win or die" cultures breed abusive leadership. *Journal of Social Issues*(74(3)), 500-528.

15 Vreja., L. O. (2016). An evolutionary perspective on toxic. *Management and Economics Review*, 217-228.

CHAPTER 3: EFFECTS AND CONSEQUENCES OF TOXIC LEADERSHIP

16 McFeely, S., & Wigert, B. (2019, March 13). From Gallup: https://www.gallup.com/workplace/247391/fixable-problem-costs-businesses-trillion.aspx

17 (n.d.). From Gallup: https://www.gallup.com/401384/indicator-hybrid-work.aspx?utm_source=linkedin&utm_medium=o_social&utm_term=gallup&utm_campaign=li-wk-indicator6_040624

18 Covey, S. M. (2008). *Speed of Trust*. Free Press

19 (2011). From Auburn University: https://harbert.auburn.edu/binaries/documents/center-for-ethical-organizational-cultures/cases/tyco.pdf

20 Shepherd, L. (2023, January 27). From Society for Human Resource Management: https://www.shrm.org/topics-tools/employment-law-compliance/class-action-lawsuits-employers-grow

21 Mackey, J. M. (2018). Leaders and followers behaving badly: A meta-analytic examination of curvilinear relationships between destructive leadership and followers' workplace behaviors. *Personal Psychology*, 3-47.

22 *Relationships Matter*. (n.d.). From www.Ohio.edu: https://www.ohio.edu/voinovich-school/blog/relationships-matter

23 Scott, D. W. (2018). Social responsibility and potential management interventions to address address employees' post-Traumatic stress. *Review of General Management*, 22-39.

24 L., W. G., & Dykes, A. C. (2019). Identifying toxic leadership & building worker resilience. *Professional Safety Journal*, 38-45.

25 Webster, V., Brough, P., & Daly, K. (2016). Fight flight or freeze: Common responses for follower coping with toxic leadership. *Stress and Health: Journal of the International Society for the Investigation of Stress*, 346-354.

26 (n.d.). From www.ukg.com: https://www.ukg.com/resources/white-paper/mental-health-work-managers-and-money

CHAPTER 4: ETHICAL LEADERSHIP

27 *The Princess Bride* (1987). [Motion Picture]. From IMDB: https://www.imdb.com/title/tt0093779/

28 Hughes, B. C. (2022). Examining Toxic Leadership: An Integrated Framework for Organizational Recovery. *Journal for Behavioral and Applied Management*, 309-344.

29 Lee, C. C., Mullins, K., & Cho, Y. S. (2016). Factors affecting the job satisfaction and retention of millennials. *Proceedings of the Academy of Organizational Culture, Communication, and Conflict*, 6-9.

30 Covella, G., Kalify, B., McCarthy, V., & Cocoran, D. (2017). Leadership's role in employee retention. *Business Management Dynamics*, 1-15.

CHAPTER 6: CULTURE RECOVERY FRAMEWORK— ORGANIZATIONAL ACCOUNTABILITY

31 Abrashoff, C. D. (2012). *It's Your Ship: Management Techniques from the Best Damn Ship in the Navy*. Grand Central Publishing.

CHAPTER 7: CULTURE RECOVERY FRAMEWORK— INDIVIDUAL ACCOUNTABILITY

32 Wiseman, L. (2017). *Multipliers, Revised and Updated: How the Best Leaders Make Everyone Smarter*. Harper Business.

33 Leitlich, A. (2016). *The Way To Coach: Leaders, Executives and Managers*.

34   Clark, T. R. (2020). *The 4 Stages of Psychological Safety: Defining the Path to Inclusion and Innovation*. Berrett-Koehler Publishers.

CHAPTER 8: CULTURE RECOVERY FRAMEWORK—INDIVIDUAL TRUST

35   Hughes, B. C. (2022). Examining Toxic Leadership: An Integrated Framework for Organizational Recovery. *Journal for Behavioral and Applied Management*, 309-344.

36   Clark, T. R. (2020). *The 4 Stages of Psychological Safety: Defining the Path to Inclusion and Innovation*. Berrett-Koehler Publishers.

37   Wiseman, L. (2017). *Multipliers, Revised and Updated: How the Best Leaders Make Everyone Smarter*. Harper Business.

CHAPTER 9: CULTURE RECOVERY FRAMEWORK— ORGANIZATIONAL TRUST

38   Dweck, D. C. (2007). *Mindset: The New Psychology of Success*. Ballantine Books.

CHAPTER 11: CASE MANAGEMENT FUNCTION

39   (n.d.). From Net Promoter System: https://www.netpromotersystem.com/about/

How to Inspire Employees From Different Generations. (n.d.). From https://trust.bizjournals.com: https://trust.bizjournals.com/blog/ what-motivates-employees-from-different-generations

Hughes, B. C. (n.d.). Consequences of Toxic Cultures.

Hughes, B. C. (n.d.). Organizational Hypocrisy.

ABOUT THE AUTHOR

As an author and speaker, Dr. Bryan C. Hughes provides thought leadership and research insights around culture recovery, toxic leadership, ethical leadership, organizational integrity, and associate retention. His extensive success in building and scaling impactful organizations is matched by his expertise in driving clear communication on strategy and operations, and human capital development. Bryan has a proven track record of leading high-performance teams, strengthening company culture, and fostering enhanced financial performance, YOY revenue growth, and net profit increases. He now works directly with organizations to support sustainable growth and performance through increasing leadership capacity, and on-purpose execution.

Bryan has nearly three decades of practical experience, with two decades in executive leadership roles. He has seen every business model and worked in several capacities, including consulting and advising organizations in every North American time zone. Through his experience, Bryan has seen the pervasive toxicity that many companies struggle to remove, and has made it his goal to help them tackle and solve this problem.

Through the academic research and practical application, he found that operational tweaks could result in minor improvements but rarely led to sustainable growth or significant change. The main blocker of operational excellence was often deeper, embedded in leadership styles and organizational culture. The result of his doctoral research created a research-backed and peer-reviewed framework—the Culture Recovery Framework outlined in this book—to heal pervasive toxicity in organizations and ultimately increase associate retention. For the past several years, Bryan has tested this framework in companies across America, successfully helping his clients heal their culture and remove toxicity.

If you would like to work with Bryan to help your organization solve for associate retention and create an ethical culture, you can contact him at bryan@cleardaystrategies.com.